OSHO

THE

ABC

OF
ENLIGHTENMENT

A SPIRITUAL DICTIONARY
FOR THE HERE AND NOW

element

Element
An Imprint of HarperCollins*Publishers*
77–85 Fulham Palace Road
Hammersmith, London W6 8JB

The website address is:
www.thorsonselement.com

and *Element* are trademarks of
HarperCollins*Publishers* Limited

First published by Element 2003
This edition published 2004

© Osho International Foundation, 2003

Excerpts from selected works by the author
OSHO is a registered trademark of
Osho International Foundation

A catalogue record for this book
is available from the British Library

ISBN 0 00 719044 1

Printed and bound in Great Britain by
Clays Ltd, St Ives plc, Bungay

THE
ABC
OF
ENLIGHTENMENT

Also by the same author

INTRODUCTION

Words are not just words. They have moods, climates of their own. When a word settles inside you, it brings a different climate to your mind, a different approach, a different vision. Call something by a different name and see how it is immediately different. So one of the most important things to remember is, if possible, live an experience and don't fix it by a word, because that will make it narrow.

You are sitting outside on a silent evening. The sun has gone and the stars are just coming out. Just be. Don't even say, 'This is beautiful,' because the moment you say that it is beautiful, it isn't the same any more. By saying 'beautiful' you are bringing in the past, and all the experiences that you said were beautiful have coloured the word. Your word 'beautiful' contains many experiences of beauty. But this experience is totally new. Life has never been like this before. It will never be again. Why bring in the past? The present is so vast, the past is so narrow. Why look through a hole in the wall when you can come out and look at the whole sky?

So try not to use words, but if you have to, be very choosy about them, because each word has a nuance of its own. Be very poetic about it. Use each word with taste, love, feeling.

There are feeling words and there are intellectual words. Drop intellectual words more and more. Use feeling words. There are political words and there are religious words. Drop political words. These are words which immediately create conflict. The moment you utter them, argument arises. So never use logical, argumentative language. Use the language of affection, of caring, of love, so that no argument arises. If you start acting this way, you will see tremendous changes.

A single word uttered without awareness can create a long chain of misery. But if you are alert, many miseries can be avoided. Just a very small change can make a lot of difference. You should be very, very careful and only use words when absolutely necessary. Avoid contaminated words. Use fresh words, non-controversial words which are not arguments, just expressions of your feelings.

If you can become a connoisseur of words, your whole life will be different. Your relationships will be totally different because 99 per cent of a relationship is expressed through words and gestures. Gestures are also words. If a word brings misery, anger, conflict, argument, drop it. What is the point of carrying it? Drop it. Replace it with something better.

The best thing is silence. Next best is singing, poetry, love.

Absolute

Never use the word 'absolute', avoid it as much as possible, because it is the word 'absolute' that creates fanatics. Nobody has the absolute truth. Truth is so vast! All truths are bound to be relative. It is the word 'absolute' that has dragged the whole of humanity into misery. The Mohammedan thinks the absolute truth is in the Koran. The Christian thinks the absolute truth is in the Bible. The Hindu thinks the absolute truth is in the Gita, and so on, so forth. And how can there be so many absolute truths? Hence the conflicts, quarrels, wars, religious crusades, jihads: 'Kill those who are claiming that their truth is absolute – *our* truth is absolute!' Down the ages, more murders, more rapes and more lootings have been commited in the name of religion than in the name of anything else. And the reason? The reason is in the word 'absolute'.

Always remember: all that we can ever know is bound to be relative.

Abstractions

It is always simple to love abstract things. It is simpler to love humanity than human beings, because in loving humanity you are not risking anything. A single human being is far more dangerous than the whole of humanity. Humanity is a word, an abstraction, there is no corresponding reality to it. A human being is reality, and when you come across reality there are going to be good times, bad times, pain, pleasure, ups and downs, highs and lows, agonies and ecstasies. Loving humanity, there will be no ecstasy and no agony. In fact, loving humanity is a way of avoiding human beings. Because you can't love human beings, you start loving humanity just to deceive yourself.

Avoid abstractions.

Absurdity

Everything beautiful is absurd. Beauty is absurd. Joy is absurd. Laughter is absurd. Love, peace, enlightenment – they are all absurd, absurd in the sense that they have no meaning beyond themselves. Their meaning is intrinsic.

Collect as many absurdities in your life as possible. The more absurdities you have, the richer you are.

Acceptance

Just for 24 hours, try it – total acceptance, whatever happens. If someone insults you, accept it, don't react, and see what happens. Suddenly you will feel an energy flowing in you that you have not felt before. Normally when somebody insults you, you feel weak, you feel disturbed, you start thinking of how to get your revenge. That person has hooked you and now you will go round and round in circles. For days, nights, months, even years, you will not be able to sleep, you will have bad dreams. People can waste a whole life over a small thing, just because someone insulted them.

Just look back into your past and remember a few things. You were a small child and the teacher in the class called you an idiot and you still remember it and feel resentment. Your father said something to you or your mother looked at you in a certain way and ever since then the wound has been there. Your parents have forgotten and even if you remind them they will not be able to remember it. Yet the wound is still open, fresh; if anybody touches it, you will explode. Don't make this wound your soul.

For 24 hours, just 24 hours, try not to react to anything, not to reject anything, whatever happens. If someone pushes you and you fall to the ground, fall! Then get up and go home. Don't do anything about it. If somebody hits you, bow your head and accept it with gratitude. Go home, don't do anything, just for 24 hours, and you will know an upsurge of energy that you have never known before, a new vitality. And once you know it, once you have tasted it, your life will be different. Then you will laugh at all the foolish things you have been doing, at all the resentments, reactions, revenges with which you have been destroying yourself.

Nobody can destroy you except you; nobody can save you except you. You are the Judas and you are the Jesus.

Acting

Acting is the most spiritual of professions for the simple reason that the actor has to identify with the act he is performing and yet remain a watcher. If he is acting Hamlet he has to become absolutely involved in being Hamlet, he has to lose himself totally in his act, and yet at the deepest core of his being he has to remain a spectator.

If he becomes absolutely identified with Hamlet, then there is bound to be trouble.

So the real actor has to live a paradox: he has to act as if he is what he is acting and yet deep down he knows he is not that. That's why I say acting is the most spiritual of professions.

Activity/Action

Remember two words: one is 'action', the other is 'activity'. Action is not activity; activity is not action. Their natures are diametrically opposite. Action is acting, responding when a situation demands it. Activity is not a response, it is when you are so restless within that you use a situation as an excuse to be active.

Action comes out of a silent mind. It is the most beautiful thing in the world. Activity comes out of a restless mind. It is the ugliest. Action has a relevance; activity is irrelevant. Action is spontaneous; activity is loaded with the past. It is not a response to the present moment, rather it is pouring your restlessness, which you have been carrying from the past, into the present. Action is creative; activity is very destructive – it destroys you, it destroys others.

Adam's apple

This gland in the throat is called Adam's apple because Adam ate the apple and he could not swallow. it. It got stuck in his throat because he was feeling divided: half of him wanted to eat and explore, and half of him was afraid. So don't create more Adam's apples – ever! Do things totally so you can swallow them and digest them.

Admiration

We want to be admired because we have no respect for ourselves. From the very beginning we are condemned by our parents, teachers, priests, politicians, the whole establishment. A single note is continuously repeated to every child: 'What you are doing is not right. You are doing what should not be done and you are not doing what should be done.' Every child is given directly and indirectly the impression that he is not really wanted, that his parents are tired, that he is somehow being tolerated, that he is a nuisance. This creates a deep wound in every one of us. To cover up that wound we seek admiration.

Adultery

The meaning – the ordinary meaning – of adultery is making love to someone you are not married to. But the real meaning of the word is making love when you are not in love. The other person may be your own husband or wife, but if you are not in love, then making love to them is adultery.

And a human being is a complex phenomenon. Today you may be in love with your wife (yes, I know it is difficult, it is hard and it is very rare too, but it happens) and then making love to her is prayer, is worship, it is communion with God. And this communion can happen even with a woman to whom you are not married, and if love is there, then it is not adultery. But if love is not there, then even what you are doing with your wife is adultery.

Advertising

The advertiser believes in the science of repetition; he simply goes on repeating that this brand of cigarette is the best. When you read it for the first time you may not believe it. But the next time, and the next, and the next – how long can you remain an unbeliever? By and by the belief will arise. And you may not even become conscious of it. It will be subliminal. Then one day when you go to a shop and the shopkeeper asks what brand of cigarette you want, you will say that brand. That repetition worked. It hypnotized you.

That's how religions have been functioning in the world – and politics too. Advertise, go on repeating the same things to the public and don't be bothered whether they believe them or not – that's not the point. Hitler says there is only one difference between a truth and a lie: the truth is a lie that has been repeated very often. And people can believe in anything; their gullibility is infinite.

Advice

Listen to advice, but don't follow it. Listen, certainly – carefully, meditatively. Try to understand what others want to convey to you. Listen, because people have great experiences, and if they are willing to share them, it will be foolish on your part not to listen. Sharing their experience may give you great insight – it will help you to become more aware – but don't follow their advice. They may be well-wishers, but if you start blindly following their advice you will remain dependent on crutches, you will always look up to others to tell you what to do, what not to do. You will always need leaders – which is a very unhealthy state to be in.

When people follow others, they become just blind. When others are giving you all that you need, why use your own eyes? When others are chewing for you, why chew on your own? When you are following others you will become weaker and weaker, more and more impoverished, more and more starved …

Real friends will not ask you to follow them but will help you to sharpen your intelligence. They won't give you fixed advice, because fixed advice is of no use. What is true today may not be true tomorrow, and what is right in one situation may be wrong in another.

Ageing

Seasons are beautiful. Through seasons every moment you become new – every moment a new mood, every moment a new nuance of being, every moment new eyes and a new face.

And who has told you that an old person is ugly? An old woman will be ugly if she is still trying to look young. Then her face will be painted, with lipstick and this and that, and then she will be ugly. But if an old woman accepts old age as natural, as it should be, then you cannot find a more beautiful face than an old face – wrinkled through many seasons, many experiences; seasoned, mature, grown up.

Alchemy

Meditate on something negative and you will be surprised: slowly sadness turns to joy, anger to compassion, greed to sharing, and so on, so forth. This is the science of inner alchemy: how to change the negative into the positive, how to change the base metal into gold.

Remember, never start with the positive, because you don't know anything about the positive. Ignore the 'positive thinkers'. They don't know anything about the inner alchemy. You don't begin with gold. If you already have gold, then what is the point of beginning at all? You don't need alchemy. So you have to begin with base metal and the base metal is what you have, is what you *are*. Hell is what you are; it has to be transformed into heaven. Poison has to be transformed into nectar. Base metal has to be transformed into gold. Start with the negative.

And once you start with the negative, you don't need to think about the positive at all. If you meditate on the negative, if you go deeply into it, to the deepest root of it, suddenly there is an explosion: the negative disappears and the positive appears. In fact the positive has always been there, hidden behind the negative. The negative was a shelter. It was needed because you were not yet worthy enough; it was needed so that you could become worthy enough to receive the positive.

Alertness

If you are alert, if your actions become more and more aware, what you do will not be done sleepily. When you start learning to drive you are alert but not efficient, because alertness takes energy and you have to be alert to many things – the gears, the wheel, the brake, the accelerator, the clutch. There are so many things you have to be aware of that you cannot be efficient, you cannot go fast. But by and by, when you become efficient, you need not be aware. You can go on humming a song or thinking about something or solving a puzzle, and the car goes by itself. The body drives it automatically. The more automatic you become, the more efficient you are.

Society needs efficiency, so it makes you more and more automatic. The whole effort of society is to make you automatic, to make you an automaton, to make you a perfectly efficient mechanism. Society doesn't bother about your awareness, in fact your awareness is a problem for society. Society doesn't want you to behave like human beings, it wants you to behave like mechanical devices, so it makes you more efficient, more productive, less aware. This is mechanization. You become efficient, but your soul is lost. The whole effort of meditation techniques is to de-automatize you, to make you alert again, to make you a human being again, not a machine.

Ambition

Ambitions are infectious. Avoid ambitious people, otherwise something of their fever is bound to infect you. You may start moving in a direction that is not yours, you may start doing things that you had never thought of before, just because you fell into company with somebody … Perhaps your father wanted you to be a doctor, so now you are a doctor. You fulfilled *his* ambition. He used you as a means to fulfil his ambition. This is not love, this is exploitation.

Ambition is the root cause of madness – try to understand your ambitiousness. Your effort to be somebody in the world will drive you mad. Just be nobody and then there is no problem. Drop ambitiousness and start living, because the ambitious person cannot live, he always postpones. His real life will always be tomorrow – and tomorrow never comes.

The ambitious person is bound to be aggressive and violent, and the violent person and aggressive person are bound to go mad. The non-ambitious person is peaceful, loving, compassionate. The ambitious person is always in a hurry, running, rushing towards something that he vaguely feels is there, but he will never find it. It is like the horizon – it does not exist, it only appears to exist. The non-ambitious person lives here and now, and to be here now is to be sane. To be totally in this moment is to be sane.

Amen

Mohammedan prayers and Christian prayers end with *amin;* Christians call it *amen,* Mohammedans call it *amin.* Hindu prayers end with *aum.* There is certainly a truth somewhere, partially expressed by all three.

When the mind becomes absolutely silent a certain sound is heard. If you are a Hindu you will interpret it as *aum,* if you are a Mohammedan as *amin,* if you are a Christian as *amen,* but nobody can say for certain what it is. In fact it can be interpreted in many ways.

Angels

Nobody believes in the sun, in the moon, because they are. People believe in God and angels and devils and this and that, because they are not. You are simply creating belief systems to cling to.

Anger

Anger is just a mental vomit. Something is wrong with what you have taken in and your whole psychic being wants to throw it out. But there is no need to throw it out onto somebody. It is because people throw anger onto others that society tells them to control it.

There is no need to throw anger on anybody. Anger just means that something is inside you that needs to be released. So you can go to your bathroom and make faces in the mirror, to unburden yourself, you can go on a long walk, you can do a little jogging and you will feel it has been released. Or you can take a pillow and beat it, fight with it, bite it until your hands and teeth are relaxed. A pillow is enlightened, a Buddha! It will not react. It will not take you to court. It will not feel any enmity towards you. It will be happy, it will laugh at you.

Within five minutes of catharsis you will feel unburdened. And once you know this you will never throw your anger onto anybody, because that is absolutely foolish.

(and)

People write to me saying, 'Somebody passed by me and I had a gut feeling that he was angry with me.' Somebody passed by you, and you have a gut feeling that he was angry with you? You could at least have asked him, 'Are you angry with me? Because I have a gut feeling …' You owe him this much courtesy at least before you determine that he is angry with you. He may not be at all interested in you, he may be angry about something else. You may give him a good laugh. But because he is angry about something, that's why you are getting the gut feeling of anger.

Another person's anger can affect you in this way. It may not be addressed to you, because emotions are not linear. They don't move from A to B, they move in circles, concentric circles. Just as when you drop a stone in the lake, concentric circles arise and go on spreading all around, when somebody is angry there are concentric circles of anger spreading around him. Anybody passing by can sense this anger. And will naturally interpret the feeling to mean that it is directed towards him.

If this happens to you, it is better to take hold of the person immediately and ask, 'What is the matter? Because I feel waves of anger around you. I don't know why, but if

11

they are addressed to me tell me, so I can do something about them. If they are not addressed to me, thank you. Go on your way and I will go on my way.'

(and)

Sometimes if you feel like being angry, be angry – there is nothing wrong in it. The problem is that if you are not angry you will not be loving. Emotions are so bound up together that if you repress anger, you will repress love also. If you repress anger, you will repress compassion also. If you release compassion, you may be afraid that you are also releasing anger. In that case you will just have to sit upon the whole pile of your emotions – and that is very uncomfortable.

Anguish

There is great anguish in every heart – the anguish of not knowing onself, the anguish of not knowing where we are coming from and where we are going to, who we are and what this life is all about. What is the meaning of life? This is our anguish, our agony. Life seems to be so futile, so utterly meaningless, a mechanical repetition. We go on doing the same things again and again – and for what? There seems to be no significance to it all. And man cannot live without experiencing some significance, without feeling that he contributes something meaningful to the world, that he is needed by existence, that he is not just a useless phenomenon, that he is not accidental, that he is required, that he is fulfilling something tremendously significant. Unless one comes to feel this, one remains on fire with anguish.

Anxiety

Anxiety means 'There is nobody to look after me. I have to carry the whole burden on my own shoulders. If I don't carry it then I am finished.' The anxious person thinks, 'Everybody is against me. Somehow, everybody is conspiring against me, everybody is at my throat. I have to protect myself. I have to be watchful, I have to plan, I have to move in such a way that I become the winner. Everybody is a competitor and they are all bent upon defeating me.'

This attitude creates anxiety, and it is the attitude of an irreligious person. When I say an irreligious person I don't mean a person who does not go to church or read the Bible – that is not the point. A person may go to church, but if he remains in anxiety he is not religious. He may be praying to God and reading the Bible just because of his anxiety. He may do it as a kind of protection, security. But such a person is not religious. He is pathological and his religion will be pathological.

The truly religious person knows nothing of anxiety; he changes the whole gestalt. He says, 'I am part of this whole existence, and if trees are not worried and the birds are not going crazy and mad and the animals are utterly happy, why can't I be? I belong to this existence, I am an essential part of it.' This trust, this understanding, this faith means that anxiety simply disappears, you have stopped creating it.

Then so much energy is released that it starts overflowing. It is so abundant, so exuberant, that life becomes a festival. It becomes a dance. Then you are religious, then you are drunk with the divine.

Apology

Ordinarily, even if we recognize that we have done something wrong, we don't try to reform ourselves, we only try to reform our image. We want everybody to recognize that it was wrong on our part but we have asked for their forgiveness and things are put right again. We want to be back on our pedestal. The fallen image is placed back on the throne. We don't reform ourselves.

You have asked forgiveness many times, but again and again you go on doing the same thing. That simply shows that it was a policy, politics, a trick to manipulate people, but you have remained the same, you have not changed at all.

If you have really asked for forgiveness, for your anger or an offence against someone, then it should not happen again. Only that can prove that you are really on the path of changing yourself.

Attachment

Attachment means clinging to something, wanting it to stay the way it is forever. That is asking for the impossible. Life is a flux, nothing remains the same.

There is so much frustration in the world because all our expectations remain unfulfilled. Each expectation brings a disaster. The young person wants to remain young forever, and that is impossible. Sooner or later he has to become old. And then old age, rather than bringing joy, brings suffering. Old age should be the very crescendo of life. It should be the highest peak, snow-covered, but if we cling to youth, it is a dark hole. We cling to the body, but the body has to go one day. Live in it, love it, respect it, take care of it, but don't become attached to it. Remember it is a *caravanserai,* an overnight stay. But in the morning we have to go.

Attention

Everyone talks about their suffering. Why is there so much emphasis on it? Why give so much attention to it? Remember the law that whatever you pay attention to grows. Attention is food – if you pay attention to something, it grows.

Now, biologists say that a child grows more if he is loved because through love he gets more attention. Even a plant grows more if a gardener pays attention to it. If it is neglected, even if everything else is given to it – the right soil, fertilizers, rain, sun; everything is given except conscious attention – it takes a longer time to grow. Now this is a scientific fact. If you love the plant and you pay attention to it, if you talk to it, if you sometimes say to it, 'I love you,' it grows faster.

So attention is the most vital thing in existence. It is a vitamin. If no one loves you, you start withering away. If no one pays attention to you, you want to die. If someone pays attention to you, you become alive again. Attention is life, *élan vital.*

If you are capable of loving yourself, if you are capable of giving attention to yourself, you will not need anyone else's attention. A Buddha can live alone on this Earth, but most people cannot. If they are alone, they will immediately commit suicide. They will say, 'What is the use? Why should I live? Who will love me? Whom shall I love?' They are not capable of loving themselves.

Babies

Every child is born in harmony. That's why babies are so beautiful. Have you ever seen a baby who is ugly? It doesn't happen. All babies are beautiful. They have a grace, a tremendous elegance which has nothing to do with practice, because they have had no time to practise anything. They come into the world without any rehearsal. They are just there, so happy, so silent, so harmonious. Such grace surrounds them, as if the whole of existence is protective towards them. Then, by and by, they learn the ways of the world and then ugliness appears. Then beautiful eyes can become horrible; then a beautiful face can become criminal; then a beautiful body can lose all grace. Then a beautiful intelligence – and every child is born intelligent; that's how things are – can become stupid, mediocre. These are human achievements.

The wrong is a human achievement, the right is divine.

Bachelorhood

I have heard about a man who searched his whole life for a perfect woman, but finally he had to die a bachelor. When he was dying, somebody said to him, 'All your life you were searching for a perfect wife. Could you not find a single woman who was perfect?'

He replied, 'Who says I didn't find her? Many times I came across a perfect woman.'

'Then what happened? Why didn't you get married?'

'Because she was looking for a perfect man!'

Baggage

As you go higher you have to drop more baggage. On the plains you can carry a lot of luggage, but when you start moving uphill you will have to decide what is unnecessary and drop it. And at a still greater altitude, even more things have to be dropped.

When Edmund Hillary reached the peak of Everest he had no luggage at all. He stood there with nothing, because everything had had to be dropped along the way. When he had started, he had so many things and so much equipment – this machine and that machine, and oxygen tanks … His was a scientific mind so there was all that luggage, with 50 servants carrying it. But by and by, at each camp something had to be dropped because it was becoming impossible to carry it. Just to carry himself was enough. Standing on Everest, he was absolutely without baggage.

On the highest peaks, one has to be weightless.

Bardo

Every person who is dying has the right to know it. Doctors go on hiding it, thinking, 'Why disturb the person?' But uncertainty disturbs; certainty, never. It is this hanging in between, this being in limbo, wondering whether you are going to live or die, that is the root cause of all worry. Once it is certain that you are going to die then there is nothing to do. One simply accepts it. And in that acceptance, a calmness, a tranquillity arises. So if people are allowed to know that they are going to die, in the moment of death they become peaceful. And whenever they become absolutely certain about death, a flame arises on their face – you can see it. In fact, a miracle happens: at that moment people become alive as never before.

In the East we have been practising that for millennia. Also, in countries like Tibet particular techniques have been developed to help people to die. They call them *Bardo Todo*. When people are dying, friends, relatives and acquaintances will gather around them to give them the absolute certainty that they are going to die and to help them to relax. Because if you can die in total relaxation, the quality of death changes and your new birth will be of a higher quality. The quality of birth is decided by death. And then, in turn, the quality of birth will decide the quality of another death. That's how you go higher and higher, that's how you evolve.

Beginners

The beginner's mind is an innocent mind, the beginner's mind is an ignorant mind. They say a Zen person always keeps the beginner's mind, he never becomes an expert. He is ready to learn. He is not closed, he is always vulnerable, he is open. Any message you bring, he is not saying from the very beginning 'I know it all.' This phrase 'beginner's mind' is of great importance.

The beginner's mind means you know you don't know. Because you know you don't know, you are ready to learn, available, open.

Behaviourism

It is no accident that psychologists go on studying rats to understand man. It may seem strange, but not really so strange as it appears, because the majority of men live like rats.

Pavlov's psychology is based on the study of dogs and Skinner's psychology is based on the study of rats. And both are perfectly true as far as the majority of humanity is concerned. Once in a while they may not be right. If they try to apply their psychology to a Buddha they may not be right, but as far as ordinary humanity is concerned they are perfectly right.

What has happened to human beings? We have lost all meaning and significance for the simple reason that we have become very cowardly. We live in such cowardly ways, we are so afraid of anything new.

Belief

Belief is fear-oriented. It is just something pseudo, painted from the outside. Belief is the cheapest thing in the world.

The believer is not a seeker. The believer does not want to seek, that's why he believes. The believer wants to avoid seeking, that's why he believes. The believer wants to be delivered, saved; he needs a saviour. He is always in search of a messiah – somebody who can eat for him, chew for him, digest for him. But if I eat, your hunger is not going to be satisfied.

Let me tell you not to believe. Even when the truth is told to you, don't believe in it! Explore, enquire, search, experiment, experience: don't believe. Even when truth is conveyed to you, if you believe in it, you turn it into a lie. A truth believed is a lie, belief turns truth into a lie.

Believe in Buddha and you believe in a lie. Believe in Christ and you believe in a lie. Don't believe in Christ, don't believe in Buddha, don't believe in me. Listen attentively, intelligently; experiment, experience. And when you have experienced, will you need to believe in anything? There will be no doubt left, so what will be the point of belief? Belief is a way of repressing doubt: you doubt, hence you need belief. The rock of belief represses the spring of doubt. When you know, you know! Your experience has expelled all darkness and all doubt. Truth is: you are full of it. Truth never creates belief.

Betrayal

There is only one betrayal and that is to betray your own life. There is no other betrayal. If you continue to live with a nagging, possessive wife or a husband without any love, you are destroying your own opportunities. In the Talmud there is the idea that after your death God will say to you, 'I gave you so many opportunities to be happy. Why didn't you take them?' He will not ask what sins you have committed, he will ask what opportunities for happiness you missed. You will be responsible for those. This is really tremendously beautiful: You will be responsible only for those opportunities that were available to you and that you missed.

Remain faithful to yourself – that is the only faith that is needed – and everything will be good.

Beyond

The beyond is the rest, the shelter. The mind is a continuous chattering, it is 24-hour chattering. Eastern psychology accepts the mind as the lowest part of human consciousness – dismal and dark. You have to go beyond it.

Beyond the mind there is peace and silence. In that peace and silence sanity is born. Enlightenment is the ultimate peak of sanity. That is when you become perfectly sane, you come to a point where silence, serenity, and consciousness are yours, 24 hours a day, waking or sleeping.

And enlightenment is not the end, because it is only concerned with individual consciousness. Individuality is still like two banks of a river. The moment the river moves into the ocean, all banks disappear, all boundaries are annihilated. You have gone beyond enlightenment.

Bibles

Who reads Bibles? Who reads Vedas? Just old people who are coming close to death and are becoming afraid – afraid that perhaps there is a God. If he asks any questions – and naturally he will ask questions – it is better to be prepared. So, to be on the safe side, look into the holy book. Read a few things here and there. If God meets you and asks a question and you can't answer, you are bound to be in trouble.

Birthdays

You are never born and never die; both are illusions. Certainly it appears that you are born, but it is just like mistaking a rope for a snake when you cannot see clearly. Night is descending, the sun has set, you are on a dark path, and suddenly you see a snake and are afraid of it. But there is only a rope lying there. Bring some light – just a candle will do – and the snake won't be there any longer. It was never there in the first place.

Birth is as illusory as the rope mistaken for a snake; and if birth is illusory, of course death is illusory too. You are

never born and you never die. You certainly enter into a
body – that is a birth – and one day you leave the body –
that's what you call death – but as far as you are concerned,
you were there before your birth and you will be there after
your death.

Blame

Mankind is in such a state of unconsciousness that whatever we do we bring more and more misery to ourselves
and to others. We go on blaming fate, we go on blaming
nature, we go on blaming society, but we never blame
ourselves.

The moment you gather enough courage to blame
yourself, the moment you accept the responsibility of who
you are, a ray of light enters into your being. You are on the
path of inner transformation.

Body

Listen to your own body. The body has a great wisdom in it.
If you listen to it, you will always be right. If you don't listen
to it and you go on forcing things on it, you will never be
happy. You will be unhappy, ill, ill-at-ease, always disturbed
and disoriented.

One of the reasons humanity is still uncivilized is the
division between mind, body and soul. This division has
been preached by all the religions of the world. They have
condemned the body, a few of them have condemned the
mind too, and they have all praised the soul. The result has
not been as they expected. It has been a very strange
poisoning of humanity. People have not dropped their
bodies, they have not dropped their minds, but they have
become guilty about them. They have lost self-respect, they

have lost touch with the wisdom of their own bodies and they have lost the mastery of their own minds. And the reality is that unless all three function in unity, we cannot be whole.

Boredom

Boredom simply means that the way you are living is wrong. Why do you feel bored? You feel bored because you have been living in accordance with dead patterns given to you by others. Renounce those patterns! Start living on your own …

The whole of humanity is bored because the person who would have been a mystic is a mathematician, the person who would have been a mathematician is a politician, the person who would have been a poet is a businessman. Nobody is in the right place; everybody is somewhere else.

So when you are bored with yourself it is because you have not been sincere with yourself, you have not been honest with yourself, you have not been respectful to your own being.

You have to take risks. Boredom can disappear in a single moment if you are ready to take risks …

Brainwashing

Everybody is afraid of brainwashing. Christians are afraid that if Christians are brainwashed they will no longer be Christians. Hindus are afraid that if Hindus are brainwashed they will no longer be Hindus. Mohammedans are afraid, communists are afraid …

I am in absolute favour of brainwashing. When I brainwash people, I find cockroaches. Cockroaches are very special animals. It has been found scientifically that wherever you find man you find cockroaches, and wherever you find cockroaches you find man. They are always together, they are the oldest companions. I am not afraid of brainwashing because I am not putting cockroaches in your mind. I am giving you an opportunity to experience a clean mind, and once you know what a clean mind is like you will never allow anybody to throw rubbish into your mind.

What is wrong with being brainwashed? Wash your brain every day, keep it clean.

Breakdown/Breakthrough

In English we have two words which are very beautiful and of great significance. One is 'breakdown', the other is 'breakthrough'. Breakdown is when your head has become absolutely meaningless to you but you don't know how to reach your heart. Your logic has become irrelevant but you don't know how to meditate. Then you break down, you go insane. But if you know meditativeness – meditativeness means the art of transforming opposites into complementaries – then there is a breakthrough: you enter into a new world, a new vision, a new perspective.

Meditation is the art of transforming madness into Buddhahood. Meditation is the art of taking you beyond logic and yet keeping your sanity intact. Meditation is the greatest discovery ever made, and I don't think there is ever going to be another discovery which can surpass meditation.

Breath

The breath is one of the most important things there is. If you are not breathing fully, you cannot live fully ... Then you will be withholding something in all that you do, almost everywhere, even in love. Even when you are talking, you will not communicate completely; something will always remain incomplete.

Everybody breathes wrongly because our whole society is based on very wrong conditions, notions, attitudes. For example, a small child is weeping and the mother tells him not to cry. What will the child do? He will start holding his breath because that is the only way to stop crying. If you hold your breath everything stops – crying, tears, everything. Then by and by that becomes fixed – don't be angry, don't cry, don't do this, don't do that. The child learns that if he breathes shallowly, he remains in control. If he breathes perfectly and totally, the way every child is born breathing, then he becomes wild. So he cripples himself.

The breathing passage has a certain musculature around it and if you have been breathing wrongly – and almost everybody has – then this musculature will have become fixed. It is as if a man has not moved for years – his legs have gone dead, his muscles have shrunk, his blood flows no more – and suddenly he decides to go for a long walk. It's a beautiful day. But he cannot move. A great deal of effort will be needed to bring those dead legs back to life. It is the same with breathing. Through deep massage, particularly through Rolfing, the muscles can relax and then you can start again. But once you do start breathing well, don't fall into your old habits again.

Breathing is life. And every change that is going to happen is going to happen through the change in your breathing. Once breathing is perfect, everything else falls into line.

Buddha

In Buddhist terminology 'Buddha' is equivalent to 'truth'. Buddhists don't talk much about truth; they talk much more about the Buddha. When you become a Buddha, you become awakened, so why talk about truth? Just ask what awakening is. Just ask what awareness is, because when you are aware, truth is there; when you are not aware, truth is not there.

A Buddha is one who lives from moment to moment, who does not live in the past, who does not live in the future, who lives in the here and now. Buddhahood is a quality of being present – and it is not a goal, you need not wait, you can become a buddha just here and now.

Bullshit

'Bullshit' is a far better word than 'rationalization', but they mean the same. 'Rationalization' is a clinical word, a word to be used by the professor. 'Bullshit' is more alive. 'Rationalization' is bloodless, 'bullshit' is very young, alive and kicking. 'Rationalization' is a philosophical term. 'Bullshit' comes from the ordinary man, from the masses, people who live on the earth, with the earth, whose hands are muddy. The word 'bullshit' is also muddy, as it is being used by people who are living the ordinary life. It does not come from the ivory towers of a university. But remember, it is more authentic, it says much more than 'rationalization'. And remember that words that are coined by professors are always anaemic. They are dead words, clinical. They do not say much. Rather than saying, they hide.

Let me put it this way: the very word 'rationalization' is a rationalization; it is being used to avoid the word 'bull-shit'.

Business

People want to remain occupied. If they have nothing to do they will find something to do. They may start reading the same newspaper again. It was rubbish in the first place, so why read it again?

Sitting alone you feel restless. You want to go to a club, to the theatre, or just to the market so that you are occupied. Everybody interested in going out, nobody is interested in going in, because the moment you think of going in you think of many things that are there, hidden. *You* have suppressed them, nobody else, so you know well that anger is there, hatred is there, sex is there, greed is there, jealousy is there ... Thousands of things are bubbling and boiling inside and any moment they can explode. So it is better to go out, not to go in. It is better to escape somewhere.

People are busy without business. They may say that they would like to rest, but nobody wants to rest because if you really rest it automatically becomes meditation and you start falling inwards. You start moving towards your inner centre and fear grips you. So you go to the market, go to a club, waste your time in thousands of different ways.

Calculation

Life can be lived in two ways, either as calculation or as poetry. We have two sides to our inner being: the calculating side, which creates science, business, politics, and the non-calculating side, which creates poetry, sculpture, music. These two sides have not yet been bridged, they have separate existences. Because of this we are immensely impoverished, we remain unnecessarily lopsided.

In scientific language it is said that your brain has two hemispheres. The left hemisphere calculates, is mathematical, is prose, and the right hemisphere is poetry, is love, is song. One side is logic, the other side is love. One side is syllogism, the other side is song. And they are not really bridged, hence we live in a kind of split.

My effort is to bridge these two hemispheres.

We should be as scientific as possible as far as the objective world is concerned and as musical as possible as far as the world of relationships is concerned.

Capitalism

Capitalism is the first system in the world which creates capital, wealth. Before, there was feudalism. It never created wealth; it exploited people, it robbed people. The wealth that the kings had was a crime. It was forcibly taken from the people, from the poor; it was not their creation.

I believe in capitalism. This is the first time in history that there has been a system which can create so much wealth that there is no need for poverty. There is no need to distribute wealth – it will be distributed automatically. There is no need for a dictatorship of the proletariat. Capitalism is perfectly in tune with democracy, with individuality, with freedom of speech. It destroys nothing.

So my approach is that we have to spread the idea of creating wealth rather than distributing it. What are you going to distribute if you don't have anything in the first place?

Capitalism is the first system which creates wealth. But nobody can eat wealth, so once you have enough, what are you going to do with the rest? There comes a point of saturation. And when capitalism reaches to the point of saturation, then there is the flowering of communism. That's why I call my community a commune. Communism, the word 'communism', comes from 'commune'.

Catharsis

Before you can reach the peaks, you have to get rid of the rubbish and the luggage that you have been carrying for lives. You have to go through a catharsis.

First, the gorilla has to be released – that is, all your repressions. To let the gorilla out of your being is the deepest cleansing, the deepest catharsis. And when all the animality has gone out of you, Buddhahood is not far away – just one step.

Buddhahood is your birthright, and the gorilla is only your conditioning. Society goes on telling you to repress things and sooner or later the repressed part of your being becomes so big that you are sitting on a volcano. It can erupt any moment. Before it erupts, it is better to release it.

So first be a gorilla – with intensity and totality. That's what happens in Dynamic Meditation: you allow your gorilla to be released without any inhibitions. Keep your gorilla inside and everybody will be happy with you, but if your gorilla is inside, you can never be at peace. I say to you, let it out. It will evaporate in the air. And what will be left behind? Pure space.

Celebration

Have you ever thought about why, all over the world, in every culture, in every society, there are just a few days in the year for celebration? These few days are just compensation, because society has taken away all celebration of life, and if nothing is given in compensation people can become a danger to the culture. Every culture has to give some compensation so that the people don't feel completely lost in misery, in sadness. But these compensations are false. The firecrackers and the lights cannot make people rejoice. They are only for children; for adults they are just a nuisance. But in a person's inner world there can be a continuous celebration, a festival of light the whole year round.

Celibacy

You can be celibate, but being celibate does not mean going beyond sexuality. The moment you were in the womb you became a sexual being. There is no way of avoiding it. So all that you can do is repress it. But then you will become unnatural and your whole life will be perverted. Repression is possible, but then transcendence is not.

Chakras

What yogis call 'the chakras' are vortexes of energy, wheels of energy. Bauls call them the seven lotuses.

We have seven chakras. With each chakra you are a different person. With the first chakra, the sex centre, you are just an animal – slightly above the animal, but not far away, just on the boundary. Below you is the animal world, above you is the world of humanity, and you are right on the boundary. That's why religions have been so against sex – because it is the highest point for animals and the lowest for man. If you remain centred at the sex chakra you are only the highest animal, nothing more.

When energy moves to the second centre, new qualities develop in you. When energy moves to the third centre, more new dimensions open to you, and so on. Finally, when the energy comes to the last centre, the seventh centre, the *sahasrar,* you transcend humanity. And unless you transcend humanity, you cannot find the ultimate. We must transcend ourselves. Only then are we fulfilled.

Challenges

The easiest is the most difficult; the difficult is not so difficult. The ego is always ready to do the difficult because in doing the difficult the ego is enhanced, it feels good. It looks like a challenge, and the ego is provoked out of its lethargy by the challenge. It fights back, it tries to conquer, it becomes aggressive. The greater the difficulty, the more aggressive the ego becomes. Aggression is its food. That's why the simple is the most difficult. The ego does not feel interested in it. The ego feels a kind of death through it. The ego cannot lose control because in losing control it will lose itself. The ego cannot lose tenseness because

31

tenseness is its very existence. If you are non-tense, if you are relaxed, the ego simply evaporates. It cannot exist in a relaxed state of consciousness; it is no longer needed.

Change

Misery arises because we don't allow change to happen. We cling, we want things to be static. If you love a woman you want her to be yours tomorrow, the same as she is today. That's how misery arises. Nobody can be certain about the next moment, what to say about tomorrow?

Life is constantly changing. Life *is* change. Only one thing is permanent, and that is change itself. To accept this changing existence with all its seasons and moods, this constant flow, which never stops for a single moment, is to be blissful.

Chaos

Chaos is always good. Order is always dead. Out of chaos stars are born; out of order, only Adolf Hitlers. So I don't have any problem with chaos. When everything is in order, it just becomes a concentration camp. Chaos has a beauty. Chaos has another name: freedom.

Charity

All the religions have been serving the poor for thousands of years and poverty still keeps on growing. Is this authentic service? If so, in thousands of years poverty should have disappeared. In fact, religion is feeding poverty.

Real service is telling the poor: 'You are being exploited and you have to revolt against vested interests.' Poverty will continue unless the poor understand that their poverty is caused by a few people who are exploiting them, sucking their blood … It is not caused by your past lives and your sins, it is caused by a social system which relies on exploitation.

Religions have to be made aware: They have been serving the poor for centuries, but what is the result? A tree is known by its fruit; if the fruit is rotten, the tree is not worth much. Serving the poor appears to be so good. It seems to be a great virtue. But service seems to be a beautiful word which is hiding an exploitative social structure.

Choicelessness

A man of pure understanding is open to all contradictions. He does not make a choice. He remains choiceless, just silently aware, knowing that there are contradictions but that ultimately they meet somewhere. Life meets death, day meets night, love meets hate, yes meets no. For the man who is beyond all opinions, yes is partial, just as no is partial. In fact, when they meet and merge into each other, when yes is no longer yes and no is no longer no, when it is all absolutely indefinable because where yes and no meet is inconceivable, this is transcendence, this is going beyond the mind.

Civilization

This idea that we have become civilized is very dangerous. It is preventing us from being civilized, because once you accept that you are civilized there is no need to work for civilization. Once you accept you are healthy, there is no need to remove any sickness that you may be suffering from. The first thing is to recognize that you are sick! Only then can something be done for your health. For centuries so-called politicians have denied that we are uncivilized, have said that we are civilized, and this camouflage prevents us from being civilized. We have completely accepted the idea that we are civilized and have forgotten that we have to see whether it is true or not. It is certainly not true.

Commandments

Moses went up the mountain. After a long time God appeared. 'Hello, Moses. Good to see you. Sorry you had to wait, but I think you will feel it was worth it because I have something very special for you today.'

Moses thought for a second and then said, 'Oh no, Lord, really. Thank you, but I don't need anything right now. Some other time perhaps.'

'Moses, this is free,' said the Lord.

'Then,' said Moses, 'give me ten!'

The Ten Commandments are all fear-oriented – don't do this, don't do that. All the commandments have failed.

And if somebody asks about my philosophical stand-point, it is not going to be that easy to answer, because I see man as a multi-dimensional being. I would have to suggest ten 'non-commandments':

1. Freedom
2. Uniqueness of individuality
3. Love
4. Meditation
5. Non-seriousness
6. Playfulness
7. Creativity
8. Sensitivity
9. Gratefulness
10. A feeling of the mysterious

These ten non-commandments constitute my basic attitude to reality, to freedom from all kinds of spiritual slavery.

Compassion
Only compassion is therapeutic, because all that is ill in human beings arises because of a lack of love. All that is wrong with man is associated somewhere with love – he has not been able to love, or he has not been able to receive love. He has not been able to share his being. That's the misery. That creates all sorts of complexes inside.

Those wounds can surface in many ways – they can become physical illness, they can become mental illness – but deep down people are suffering from lack of love. Just as food is needed for the body, so love is needed for the soul. The body cannot survive without food and the soul cannot survive without love.

Concentration
Concentration has tunnel vision. Have you ever looked into a tunnel? From one side, where you are looking from, it is big. But if the tunnel is two miles long, the other side is just a small round light, nothing else. The longer the tunnel, the smaller the other end. You have to focus, and focusing is always a tense affair.

Concentration is not natural to the mind. The mind is a vagabond. It enjoys moving from one thing to another. It is always excited by the new. In concentration, the mind is almost imprisoned.

In the Second World War, they started calling the places where they were keeping prisoners 'concentration camps'. They meant they were bringing all kinds of prisoners together and concentrating them in one place. But concentration is actually bringing together all the energies of your mind and body and putting them into a narrowing hole. It is tiring.

Conscience

Society has put its own ideas inside you and they function as your conscience. They don't allow your real conscience to surface; they don't allow your own consciousness to come and take charge of your life.

Society is very political. Outside it has posted the policeman and the magistrate; inside it has posted the conscience, the inner policeman, the inner magistrate. And it is not even satisfied with this arrangement – above, it has posted a god, the super-policeman, the chief constable. He is up there looking down on you; even in your bathroom he is watching you. Somebody is following you continuously, you are never left alone just to be yourself.

Consciousness

Say you go for a morning walk. In a way you are moving, in a way you are not moving. Your body is moving, your mind is moving, but your consciousness is still the same. You were a child, then you were young, then you grew old. Everything has moved and yet nothing has moved; your consciousness is still the same.

That's why it is very difficult, if you don't keep a record, if you don't have a birth certificate, if you don't have a calendar, to judge your age. If you close your eyes and try to figure out how old you are, you will not be able to figure it out at all …

If you are shown a picture of yourself taken the first day in your mother's womb, you will not be able to believe that it is you. Do you think you will be able to recognize yourself? You will be just a dot, almost invisible to the naked eye; you will need a microscope to see yourself. And since then … But all those changes are peripheral; at the centre you are still the same. Nothing has changed, nothing ever changes.

When you go for a morning walk tomorrow, watch: your body moves, but something in you remains unmoving.

Contraception

Contraceptives have transformed the very quality of sex: it has become fun. Sex is no longer so serious as it used to be. It has become just playfulness – two bodies playing with each other, that's all. There is nothing wrong in it. You play football – what is wrong in that? You play volleyball – what is wrong in that? And sex is also a game.

Now religions are bound to be afraid, because contraceptives can undermine their whole edifice. What atheists could not do in centuries, contraceptives can do within decades. They have already done it: contraceptives have made people free of the priest.

Courage

Courage is risking the known for the unknown, the familiar for the unfamiliar, the comfortable for the uncomfortable, arduous pilgrimage to some unknown destination. We never know whether we will be able to make it or not. It is gambling, but only gamblers know what life is.

Creativity

Creativity has nothing to do with any particular work. Creativity has everything to do with the quality of consciousness. Whatever you do can become creative, if you know what creativity means.

Creativity means enjoying any work as meditation; doing any work with deep love. If you love me and you clean this auditorium, it is creative. If you don't love me, then of course it is a chore, it is a duty to be done somehow, it is a burden. Then you have to be creative some other time. What will you do in that other time? Can you find something better to do? Do you think that if you paint, you will feel creative? But painting is just as ordinary as cleaning the floor. You will be throwing colours onto a canvas. Here you are washing the floor. What is the difference?

When you are talking to a friend, you may feel time is being wasted and you are not being creative. If you were writing a great book instead, then you would be creative. But if a friend has come to see you, a little gossiping is perfectly beautiful. Be creative.

Dance

Dance is an experiment, an experiment to bring your body, your mind and your soul in tune. Dance is one of the most rhythmic phenomena. If you are really dancing, there is no other activity which creates such unity. If you are sitting, you are not using your body, you are only using your mind. If you are running very fast, if your life is in danger, you are only using your body, you are not using your mind. If you are dancing you are neither sitting nor running for your life. Dance is movement, a joyful movement. The body is moving, the energy is flowing, the mind is moving, the mind is flowing. And when these are all flowing they melt into each other. You become psychosomatic. A certain alchemy starts happening.

Danger

In dangerous situations the mind stops automatically. Why? Because the mind is a mechanism and it can only do the routine things which it has been trained to do.

You cannot train your mind for accidents, otherwise they would not be called accidents. If you are ready for them, if you have passed through rehearsals, then they will not be accidents. 'Accident' means something that the mind is not ready for, something so sudden, leaping from the unknown, that the mind cannot do anything. It is not ready, it is not trained for accidents. It is bound to stop unless you start doing something else, something for which you are trained …

That is why danger has a secret appeal, an intrinsic appeal. Moments of danger are meditative moments. If you race a car and it goes beyond 90 miles per hour and then beyond 100 and then beyond 110 and beyond 120, a situation arises in which anything can happen and you will not be able to do anything about it. Now the car is really beyond your control. Suddenly the mind cannot function; it is not ready for this situation. That is the thrill of speed – the mind stops, silence creeps in, you are thrown to the centre.

Death

Think of a life without death – it would be an unendurable existence. It is impossible to live without death. Death defines life, gives it a kind of intensity. Because life is fleeting, each moment becomes precious. If life were eternal, who would care? You could wait for tomorrow forever, so who would live here and now? But because tomorrow there is death, it forces you to live here and now. You have to plunge into the present moment, you have to go to its ultimate depth, because who knows, the next moment may come or may not come.

Seeing this rhythm, you can be at ease, at ease with both life and death. When unhappiness comes, you welcome it, when happiness comes, you welcome it, knowing that they are partners in the same game.

This is something which has to be remembered continuously. If it becomes a fundamental remembrance in you, your life will have a totally new flavour – the flavour of freedom, the flavour of non-attachment. Whatever happens, you will remain still, silent, accepting.

Depression

Whenever you are depressed, wait for the moment when the depression goes. Nothing lasts forever; the depression will go. And when it leaves you, be aware and alert, because after the depression, after the night, there will be dawn and the sun will rise. If you can be alert in that moment, you will he happy that you were depressed. You will be grateful that you were depressed, because it was only through your depression that this happiness was possible.

But what do we do? We move in an infinite regression We get depressed. Then we get depressed because of the depression: a second depression follows. If you are depressed, that's OK! There is nothing wrong in it. It is beautiful because through it you will learn and mature. But instead you feel bad. 'Why do I get depressed? I should not get depressed.' Then you start fighting with the depression. The first depression is good, but the second depression is unreal. And this unreal depression will cloud your mind. You will miss the dawn that would have followed the real depression.

When you are depressed, be depressed. Simply be depressed. Don't get depressed about your depression. Don't fight it, don't create any diversions, don't force it to go. Just allow it to happen. It will go by itself. Life is a flux; nothing remains the same. You are not needed; the river moves by itself, you don't have to push it. If you are trying to push it, you are foolish. The river flows by itself. Allow it to flow.

Destination

To accept life in its totality, as it is, means to relax and let life take charge of you, then wherever it takes you, go with it, go to your destination.

A man with this attitude is always at peace. Nothing that happens is a problem for him, he simply goes with it. Not only does he have no resistance, but he welcomes life in whatever form it takes. He welcomes death – even death cannot disturb him. Nothing can disturb him, because he goes along with everything, he allows it ...

He is just like a leaf dropping from a tree. If the wind takes it up, it goes up; if the wind takes it to the north, it goes to the north; if the wind takes it to the south, it goes to the south; if the wind drops it on the ground, it rests on the ground. It does not say to the wind, 'This is very contradictory – you just started going north, and now you have started going south. I don't want to go south, I am destined for the north.' No, the leaf has no destination of its own.

Existence has its own destination, and the man of meditation makes existence's destination his own destination.

Destructiveness

If you don't use your energy in a creative way, if it doesn't become dance and laughter and delight, then it will become harmful and poisonous. It will be destructive.

It is said that Adolf Hitler wanted to become a painter, but he was refused admission to the academy. Just think, the whole world would have been totally different if he had been accepted. There would have been no Second World War. History would have been totally different. This man wanted to be creative and he had the energy – he had tremendous energy; he dragged the whole world towards destruction as no other man has ever been able to do – but the energy which could have become creative became destructive.

Devil

In the Garden of Eden Eve is persuaded by the Devil to eat from the Tree of Wisdom. Eve is naturally afraid – God has prohibited it – but the reasoning that convinces her is very significant. The Devil says, 'God has prohibited the two most significant experiences, wisdom and immortality, because he is very jealous. If you are also enlightened, and you are also immortal, you will become a god in your own right. And he wants to remain the only god and does not want anybody else to attain that position.'

I am surprised that nobody has appreciated the Devil, because what he is saying here is significant. The Devil was the first great revolutionary. He himself used to be an angel, but because he had the mind of a revolutionary he was thrown out of the company of God, condemned as evil. But the way he persuaded Eve makes me respect him. He is teaching exactly what all the enlightened people of the world have been teaching: that you can become a god. You are essentially a god, it is just that you have forgotten it. You are asleep and you don't know who you are. All that you need is an awakening.

Adam and Eve ate the fruit from the Tree of Wisdom, but they were not quick enough to eat from the other tree too. They were caught red-handed on the first tree. That is the sad part of it.

Devotion

Devotion is a quality in your heart. You feel full of reverence for everything that is. You feel a great love for all that is. It is not a question of whether the person is worthy of it or not, because love is not a business. It is not a question of whether a person is worthy or not, the question is whether your heart is overflowing with love or not. If it is overflowing, it will reach those who are worthy, it will reach those who are unworthy. It will not discriminate at all.

The clouds are full and they shower. Do you think the rain falls on good people only and avoids bad people, that it falls only on good Christians, good Hindus, good Jews and it simply does not fall on atheists? Rain simply showers because the clouds are so full.

Devotion is overflowing love.

Discipline

Discipline is simply a way of becoming more centred, more alert, more aware, more meditative; not functioning through the head, not even through the heart, but functioning from the very core of your being, from the very innermost core, from the centre of your being, from all of your being. It is not a reaction – reaction comes from the past – it is a *response*. Response is always *in* the present, *to* the present.

Zen gives you the discipline to become a mirror so that you can reflect that which is. All that is needed is an awareness without thought.

Disobedience

Disobedience is not a sin, disobedience is part of growth. Each child has to disobey his parents sooner or later – and the sooner the better, because life is short. You should not waste your time. You have to learn to say 'no'; only then does a point arise where you can say 'yes'. Without being able to say 'no', nobody is capable of saying 'yes'. Disobedience is the background against which real obedience blossoms.

Doubt

Doubt sharpens your intelligence. It is a challenge. You are neither saying 'yes' nor saying 'no'. You are saying only one thing: 'I am ignorant, and I am not going to trust unless I have experienced, whatever the case, unless I arrive at something which is indubitable.'

Doubt is something of tremendous significance. Only those who have doubted to the very end have found what truth is, what love is, what silence is, what beauty is. Scepticism finds nothing. It is utterly empty, but it makes a lot of noise. Empty drums make a lot of noise. And you cannot argue with a sceptic because he will go on saying 'no' to anything that you cannot place as an object before him.

But doubt, though it is a long way and a hard way, goes on eliminating all that is not true. Ultimately only that which is true remains. And nobody can deny truth when they are facing it, experiencing it. It is not a belief. You have searched, gone into great anxiety, anguish, despair. There were many moments when you wanted to stop, because it looked as if the journey was endless. It is not. There is an end; you just have to keep going.

Doubt is surgical – it cuts out all that is absurd. But finally the real remains, unclouded. Doubt removes the clouds.

Dreams

Dream analysis cannot help you to become enlightened, but dream witnessing can certainly help you.

That is the difference between psychology and religion: psychology analyses dreams; religion watches them, helps you to become aware of them. And the moment you become aware of your dreams they disappear; they can't exist for a moment longer. They can exist only when you are utterly unaware; that is an absolute condition of their existence.

A Buddha never dreams, he cannot dream. Even if he wants to dream he cannot. Dreaming simply disappears from his being because even in the night while he is asleep, deep down in his innermost core he is awake.

There are night dreams and there are daydreams. You simply change from one dream to another dream, one kind of dream to another kind of dream.

Remember who is seeing the dreams. Awake to that witness. Don't pay much attention to the dreams themselves.

Duty

Whenever the question arises of what has to be done, this has to be the criterion: if it brings joy, do it. Whatever brings joy to you will bring joy to others too. Sometimes it may not be very apparent, but this is the fundamental law: that which brings joy to you is bound to bring joy to every-body, and that which brings misery to you is bound to create misery for others, sooner or later. Be utterly self-full, and remember that in being self-full, you are serving humanity. There is no other service. All that goes on in the name of duty is ugly. Duty is a dirty four-letter word – avoid it! Do things out of joy but never out of duty.

Ecology

Ecology is very good. Work for it, but look for the inner ecology also. Because as I see it, the outer ecology is being destroyed because the inner ecology has been destroyed. It is just an outcome. When a man is no longer whole inside – divided, in conflict, like a fighting mob, a crowd – that man creates disturbance in nature also. And these are related.

When nature is destroyed, then mankind is destroyed even more. Then again nature goes on affecting mankind and mankind goes on affecting nature. It is a vicious circle. But as I see it, the basic problem is somewhere inside mankind. If you are relaxed inside, if you have come to a settlement with your own nature, then you will be able to understand the natural functioning of the world and you will not create any problems for it. You will not create any gap in it. You will see that everything is interconnected. But the basic problem is in mankind.

Economics

We know only one kind of economics: worldly economics. If you give your money, you will lose it. You have to cling on to it. You have to snatch it away from others. You have to give less and get more, then you are in profit.

But inner economics is totally different, just the polar opposite of the outer: the more you give, the more you have; the less you give, the less you have; the more you give, the more the whole of existence goes on pouring into you. You have to be constantly giving, sharing for the sheer joy of sharing.

It needs guts, but once you have experienced it, once you have come to know the inner mathematics, then there is no problem. The first step needs courage, after that there is no problem at all. Once you know that the more you give, the more you get, then it is very easy.

The first step in love cannot be taken by a coward. It needs somebody bold in spirit who can take a risk, because in the beginning it is a risk. Who knows whether you will get any response or not? Who knows? You may give your love and nothing may come in return. There is no guarantee. But that first step has to be taken in trust, then the second step is very easy and you can move thousands of miles. Then there is no problem at all; then the whole journey is very simple and life becomes richer and richer at each step.

Ecstasy

Ecstasy is a language that we have completely forgotten. We have been forced to forget it; we have been compelled to forget it. Society is against it, civilization is against it. Society has a tremendous investment in misery. It depends on misery, it feeds on misery, it survives on misery. Society is not for human beings. Society is using human beings as a means for its own ends. Society has become more important than humanity. Culture, civilization, the church, they all have become more important. They were meant to be for man, but now they have almost reversed the whole process; now man exists for them.

Every child is born ecstatic. Ecstasy is natural. It is not something that happens only to great sages, it is something that everybody brings with them into the world. It is life's innermost core. It is part of being alive. Life is ecstasy ...

Education

What we call education is not education at all, it is just the opposite of education. The very word 'education' means drawing something out that is within, bringing a person's centre to the surface, to the circumference, bringing their latent, unmanifest, dormant being into manifestation, making it active, dynamic. That's what education is.

But this is not happening in the name of education. In the name of education just the opposite is happening: everybody is being stuffed with ideas. Nothing is being drawn out of the well; the waters of the well are not being drawn, instead rocks are being thrown into the well. Soon the water will disappear; the well will be full of rocks. And that's a scholar, a pundit, a professor. They are nothing but stuffed tomatoes, stuffed potatoes – nothing else, just stuffed people, stuffed with all kinds of bullshit.

Ego

Everybody is born without an ego. When a child is born, he is simply consciousness: floating, flowing, lucid, innocent, virgin. No ego exists. By and by, the ego is created – by others. The ego is the accumulated effect of others' opinions. Somebody comes, a neighbour, and says, 'What a beautiful child,' and looks at the child with a very appreciative look. Now the ego starts functioning. Somebody smiles, somebody else doesn't smile; sometimes the mother is very loving, sometimes she is very angry. And the child is learning that he is not accepted as he is. He is not accepted unconditionally. If he cries and weeps when visitors are in the house, then his mother is very angry. If he cries and weeps when there are no visitors, his mother doesn't bother. If he does not cry and weep at all, his mother awards him with a loving kiss and caress. When visitors are there, if he can keep quiet, his mother is tremendously happy and rewards him. He is learning others' opinions about himself; he is looking into the mirror of relationship.

You cannot see your face directly. You have to look in a mirror. That reflection becomes your idea of your face, and there are a thousand and one mirrors all around you. They all reflect you. Somebody loves you, somebody hates you, somebody is indifferent to you. And by and by, the child grows and as he grows he goes on accumulating the opinions of others. The total essence of the opinions of others is the ego.Then he starts looking at himself the way others look at him. Then he starts looking at himself from the outside – that's what ego is. If people appreciate and applaud him, then he thinks that he is perfectly beautiful, accepted. If people don't applaud and don't appreciate him, but reject him, he feels condemned. Then he goes on seeking ways to be appreciated, to be assured again and again that he is worthy, that he has meaning and significance. Then he becomes afraid to be himself. He has to fit in with the opinion of others.

If you drop the ego, suddenly you become a child again. Now you are not worried about what others think of you, now you don't pay any attention to what others say about you. You are not concerned, not even a bit. Now you have dropped the mirror. It is pointless – you have your face, why ask the mirror what it looks like?

Emptiness

Whenever we hear the word 'empty' we think of something negative. In Buddha's language, emptiness is not negative; it is absolutely positive, more positive than your so-called fullness, because emptiness is full of freedom. Everything else has been removed. Emptiness is spacious; all boundaries have been dropped. It is unbounded – and only in unbounded space is freedom possible. Buddha's emptiness is not ordinary emptiness; it is not only the absence of something, it is the presence of something invisible.

For example, when you empty your room, as you remove the furniture and the paintings, the room becomes empty on the one hand because nothing is left inside, but on the other hand, something invisible starts filling it. That is 'roominess', spaciousness; the room becomes bigger. As you remove more and more things, the room becomes bigger and bigger. When everything is removed, even the walls, then the room is as big as the whole sky.

That's the whole process of meditation: removing everything; removing yourself so totally that nothing is left behind – not even you. In that utter silence there is freedom.

Energy

Just watch yourself and you will not find a single self in you but many selves. You are multi-psychic, you have many minds, and each mind is fighting with the other minds. There is great competition inside you, a continual quarrel.

And in that quarrel, in that conflict, you are dissipating energy; and when you dissipate energy in constant civil war you lose the zest for life. You lose every possibility of being ecstatic, you lose joy.

William Blake is right when he says, 'Energy is delight.' That's a very profound statement. Yes, energy *is* delight, and the greater your energy, the greater your delight. It is energy that becomes delight; overflowing energy is delight, overflowing energy becomes celebration. When energy is dancing in you, in unison, in deep harmony, in rhythm and flow, you become a blessing to the world.

Enlightenment

Enlightenment is simply the process of becoming aware of your unconscious layers of personality and dropping those layers. They are not you; they are false faces. And because of those false faces, you cannot discover your original face. Enlightenment is nothing but the discovery of the original face – the essential reality you brought with you and the essential reality you will take with you when you die. All the layers gathered between birth and death will be left behind you.

When you become enlightened, you don't become a new person. In fact you don't gain anything, you lose something: you lose your chains, you lose your bondage, you lose your misery, you go on losing. Enlightenment is a process of losing. When there is nothing left to lose, there is nirvana. That state of utter silence can be called enlightenment ...

I don't promise you anything. I don't promise you the kingdom of God, I don't promise you enlightenment. I don't make any promises at all. My whole approach is of living moment to moment, living moment to moment joyously, ecstatically, living moment to moment totally, intensely, passionately … Enlightened or unenlightened, what does it matter?

If you live passionately, your ego dissolves. If you are total in your acts, your ego is *bound* to dissolve. It is like when a dancer goes on and on dancing – a moment comes when only the dance remains and the dancer disappears. That is the moment of enlightenment.

Whenever the doer is not there, the manipulator is not there; whenever there is nobody inside you and there is only emptiness, nothingness, that is enlightenment. And whatever is born out of that beautiful space has grace, has glory.

Equality

Every individual is born with some specific talent, some specific genius. A person may not be a poet like Shelley or Rabindranath Tagore, or a painter like Picasso or Rembrandt, or a musician like Beethoven or Mozart, but everyone must have *something*. Nobody comes without a gift; everybody brings a certain potential. But the idea of equality is dangerous, because the rose has to be the rose and the marigold has to be the marigold and the lotus has to be the lotus. If you start trying to make them equal then you will destroy them all; the roses, the lotuses, the marigolds, all will be destroyed. You can succeed in creating plastic flowers which will be equal to each other, but they will be dead.

Escapism

Life has to be used as an opportunity to become more conscious, more crystallized, more centred and rooted. If you escape, it will be as if a seed escapes from the soil and hides in a cave where there is no soil, only stones. There the seed will be safe. In soil, the seed will have to die, disappear. When the seed disappears, the plant sprouts. Now the danger starts. Now the whole world seems to be against the beautiful green sprout: winds come and try to uproot it, clouds come, thunderstorms come, there are children and there are animals and there are gardeners, and millions of problems to be faced, and the small plant is fighting alone. The seed was living comfortably, there were no problems, no wind, no soil, no animals – nothing was a problem. The seed was protected, secure; it was completely closed into itself.

If you go to a cave in the Himalayas, you will become a seed. You won't sprout.

Those winds of adversity are not blowing against you; they give you an opportunity, they give you a challenge, they give you the chance to get deeply rooted. They tell you to stand your ground and fight a good fight. They make you strong.

Esotericism

Just as some people like detective novels, so others are interested in esoteric knowledge. But a really religious person has nothing to do with esotericism.

There is nothing esoteric in existence. Existence is nude, naked; nothing is hidden …

Spirituality is experience, not knowledge. You cannot reduce it to knowledge; it is always knowing, never knowledge. It is an insight, it cannot be put into words. You cannot put it into theories, into systems of thought; that is impossible. And those who try to do it don't know anything

… This is a strange phenomenon: those who know never try to reduce their knowing to knowledge, and those who don't know can create any knowledge, any esoteric system, any invention.

All spiritual knowledge is the invention of the mind. Real spiritual *knowing* happens only when the mind has been dropped, when you are in a state of no-mind.

Eternity

This word *kala* in Sanskrit is very meaningful: one meaning is 'time', another meaning is 'death'. The same word means time and death. It is beautiful, because time *is* death. The moment you enter time, you are ready to die. With birth, death has entered you. A birthday is also a deathday. When a child is born, he has entered the realm of death. Now only one thing is certain: that he will die. Everything else is just uncertain; it may happen, it may not happen. But the moment a child is born, the moment he takes his first breath, it is absolutely certain that he will die.

Entering life is entering death; entering time is entering death.

Eternity is deathlessness. How can we find eternity? What is the way? We have to understand the process of time.

The process of time is horizontal: one moment passes, then another comes; that passes, then another comes – a procession of moments, a queue of moments. One passes, then another comes; another passes, then another comes. It is horizontal.

Eternity is vertical: you go deep into the moment, not moving in a line but into depth. You drown yourself in the moment.

Ordinarily we are standing on the bank of time. The river goes on passing by; one moment, another moment, and another, and the sequence of moments continues. This is how we ordinarily live; this is how we live in time.

Then there is another way – to jump into the river, drown in the moment, in the here and now. Then suddenly, time stops. Then you are moving in an altogether different dimension, the vertical dimension. That is eternity. That is the meaning of Jesus' cross.

The cross is a time symbol. It is made of two lines: one vertical, one horizontal. On the horizontal line there are the hands of Christ and on the vertical line there is his whole being. Hands are symbolic of action: doing, having. Having is in time; being is in eternity. So whatever you *do* is in time, whatever you *are* is in eternity. Whatever you achieve is in time, whatever is your nature is in eternity. Change from having and doing to being. You can do it now. This very moment, if you forget past and future, then time stops. Then nothing moves, then everything is absolutely silent and you start drowning in the here and now. That 'now' is eternity.

Evil

The Lord's Prayer says, 'Lead us not into temptation, but deliver us from evil.'

There is no evil, hence there is no need to be delivered from anything. There is only one thing and that is a state of unconsciousness, unknowing, unawareness. I will not call it 'evil' – it is a situation, a challenge, an adventure, it is not evil. Existence is not evil, existence is an opportunity to grow. And, of course, the opportunity to grow is possible only if you are tempted in thousands of ways, if you are called forth by unknown aspirations, if a tremendous desire in you arises to explore ... And the only thing that can prevent you is unconsciousness, unawareness. That too is a great challenge – to conquer your unconsciousness, your unawareness.

Become more conscious, become more aware, become more alive. Let all your juices flow. Don't hold back. Respect your nature, love yourself and don't be worried about unnecessary things. Unworried, move into the thick of life, explore it. Yes, you will commit many mistakes – so what? You learn through committing mistakes. Yes, you will commit many errors – so what? It is only by committing errors that you come to the right door. Before you knock at the right door, you have to knock on thousands of wrong doors. That is part of the game, part of the play.

Evolution

Evolution was not discovered by Charles Darwin. Evolution is an Eastern concept discovered by mystics – and in the East they have really gone into it more deeply. Charles Darwin was only superficial; he thought that man came from monkeys and he was laughed at all over the world. The mystic does not say that man came from monkeys, but that the essence of consciousness has passed through many forms, and it has passed through the forms of monkeys too.

I was really shocked by Ronald Reagan's government. They tried to prohibit universities and colleges and schools from teaching Charles Darwin's theory of evolution because it went against the Christian idea of creation. The Christian idea was that God created everything. He created monkeys as monkeys and created men as men. He made the world perfect. So monkeys did not evolve into men.

Evolution would only have been possible only if things had
been imperfect.

The American Constitution makes it clear that religion
should not interfere with people's lives, particularly via
government powers: government should be neutral. To
stop the whole of America from knowing anything about
Charles Darwin and his theory of evolution is dangerous. I
am not saying Charles Darwin is right or wrong; that is not
my business. I am saying that the idea of evolution should
not be taken away from people's minds. In fact, they
should be made aware that for thousands of years we have
not been evolving and we *should* evolve.

Existence

Existence is paradoxical; paradox is its very core. It exists
through opposites, it is a balance of opposites. A person
who learns how to balance becomes capable of knowing
what life is, what existence is, what godliness is. The secret
key is balance.

Existence is a mystery because you can go on finding
answers, but finally you cannot answer the ultimate question. And it is not far away; it soon comes up. And in
answer to the ultimate question, I have not yet come across
a single person in the whole history of the world who has
had the courage to say 'I don't know.'

Existentialism

Why did existentialism become the most important philosophical movement in Europe? For the simple reason that
Europe was affluent, rich. And when you are rich, paradise
means nothing to you. What can paradise give you which
Paris cannot give?

And when you have all that you can desire, suddenly you become aware that something is missing: the meaning. The existentialists had everything, but that black hole of anguish inside was not diminished; it became clearer in contrast to all the riches and all the comforts and all the luxuries. Then they realized that nothing could help.

A tremendous helplessness – that is anguish. An ultimate hopelessness – that is despair.

But I don't think these people were really existentialist in my sense of the word. They were just reacting against the past, against the hope for great things. Science had brought everything which people had longed for for centuries and it had not brought contentment. It had not brought fulfilment. The rich were poorer than the poor. The poor at least have hope; existentialists don't even have hope.

In my definition, existentialism is not an 'ism'. It is unfortunate that I have to use the language that is available; otherwise I would not call it 'ism'. That suffix stinks.

Meditation is the only existentialist approach. It is the only way to existence. Jean-Paul Sartre never heard about meditation. Kierkegaard had no idea what meditation was.

Meditation is simply to be totally in the present and to be in rhythm with the existence that surrounds you. It is not intellectual, it is total: your whole being is involved in it. And if even for a moment you can taste the wine of existence, that transforms your whole life.

Experience

Never lose an opportunity which can give you something unfamiliar. Never cling to the past, always remain open, ready to walk a path which you have never walked before. Who knows? Even if it proves useless, it will be an experience.

Experimentation

I am neither a politician nor a religious leader. I teach a whole life, a total life. An atheist can be with me, a Christian can be with me, a Jew can be with me. I don't make any distinctions. No nations, no religions, no distinctions. And I don't say that to be with me you have to believe anything. I say, experiment, and if you find something is true, then it is up to you whether to believe it or not. But I am not the one to give you a faith. I can give you only a method of enquiry, a method of experimentation.

Exploration

Life is exploration, life is adventure.

Everyone has to explore in their own way. This is the only golden rule there is. There is no superhighway with milestones telling you how far you are from the goal. In spiritual exploration, you have to create your path by walking it; there is no path ready-made for you. And my feeling is that this is tremendously blissful and ecstatic.

You are not like railway trains. If you are running on rails, like a train, you cannot run into the jungles if you want to, or into the mountains. You cannot run anywhere you like. The railway train is a prisoner. But a river is not a prisoner. It can also travel a long way. It may travel thousands of miles, from the Himalayas to the ocean, with no map, no guidelines, no guides, and nobody to ask 'Which way am I to go now?', because each step is a crossroads. But strangely enough, every river reaches the ocean with great freedom, finding its own path.

Faith

Faith is only for the blind.

Faith is for the blind; trust is for one who has tasted something of the ultimate. The faithful are the followers. I don't want anybody to believe or to have faith. I want you to trust in yourself.

This distinction has to be remembered. Belief is always belief in somebody else's ideology, and faith is faith in somebody else's personality.

Faith is not a virtue, and it is not a great contribution to humanity's evolution. Faith is the greatest hindrance in people's search for truth. Before you go in search you have already been handed a secondhand dirty faith and you are told that just this much is enough. You don't have to search, Jesus has done it for you, Buddha has done it for you.

Faith simply means hiding ignorance, and it is very cheap. Truth needs great energy, great urgency and a total involvement in the search.

Truth is within you, faith comes from outside. Anything that comes from outside is not going to help you.

Fanaticism

Only a man who has doubt within himself becomes a fanatic. A fanatic Hindu is one who does not really trust that Hinduism is right. A fanatic Christian is one who has doubts about Christianity. He becomes fanatic, aggressive, not to prove anything to others, but to prove to himself that he really believes.

When you really know something, you are not a fanatic at all.

Fantastic

Two women are talking in a tearoom at four o'clock over large gooey ice-cream sundaes and little sugary cakes. They have not seen each other since school and one is bragging about her very advantageous marriage.

'My husband buys me whole new sets of diamonds when the ones I have get dirty,' she says. 'I never even bother to clean them.'

'Fantastic!' says the other woman.

'Yes,' says the first, 'we get a new car every two months. None of this hire-purchase stuff! My husband buys them outright, and we give them to the gardener and houseman and people like that for presents.'

'Fantastic!' says the other.

'And our house,' pursues the first, 'well, what's the use of talking about it? It's just …'

'Fantastic!' finishes the other.

'Yes, and tell me, what are you doing nowadays?' says the first woman.

'I go to charm school,' says the other.

'Charm school? Why, how quaint! What do you learn there?'

'Well, we learn to say "Fantastic" instead of "Bullshit"!'

Fear

When you are afraid, be afraid! Why create a duality? When moments of fear come, be fearful, tremble with fear, allow fear to take possession of you …

When fear comes, tremble like a leaf in a strong wind. And it will be beautiful. When it has gone you will feel so serene and calm, as when everything is left calm and quiet after a strong storm. Why be always fighting something? Fear comes – it is natural, absolutely natural. To think of a man without fear is impossible, because he would be dead …

Fear is part of your intelligence, there is nothing wrong in it. Fear simply shows there is death, and we human beings are here only for a few moments. The trembling says that we are not going to be here permanently, we are not here eternally, just a few days more and you will be gone.

Only one thing is to be understood: when you allow yourself to feel fear and you tremble, watch it, enjoy it, and in that watching you will transcend it, you will see your body is trembling, you will see your mind is trembling, but you will come to feel a point within you, a deep centre, which remains unaffected. The storm passes by, but somewhere deep within you there is a centre which is untouched: the centre of the cyclone.

Feeling

Think less, feel more. Intellectualize less, intuit more. Thinking is a very deceptive process, it makes you feel that you are doing great things. But you are simply making castles in the air. Thoughts are nothing but castles in the air.

Feelings are more material, more substantial. They transform you. Thinking about love is not going to help you, but feeling love is bound to change you. Thinking is very much loved by the ego, because the ego feeds on fictions. The ego cannot digest any reality, and thinking is a fictitious process …

Change from the mind to the heart, from thinking to feeling, from logic to love.

Feminine

Respect the feminine – it is higher, certainly higher, than the masculine qualities. But the male chauvinist mind is incapable of accepting it. Out of an inferiority complex the male mind has tried to repress the feminine and of course because the male is aggressive, violent, destructive, he can repress it. The feminine is receptive, surrendering; it knows how to let go, it knows how to adjust, so it has become adjusted even to the male chauvinist attitude.

The whole past of humanity is ugly and the reason why is that we have not allowed the feminine qualities to blossom.

So become more and more receptive, sensitive, creative, loving, dancing, singing – and that's how you will go on becoming more and more meditative. And the more meditative you are, the more you will find feminine qualities blossoming in you.

Followers

All followers are lost.

It even happens to great intellectuals. Martin Heidegger, one of the greatest intellectuals of this age, was a follower of Adolf Hitler. And after Hitler's defeat and the exposure of his brutality, murderousness and violence, even Heidegger shrank back and said, 'I was simply following the leader of the nation.'

A follower is just finding ways and means to protect himself, to be secure. A follower is trying just to throw responsibility onto somebody else's shoulders. The follower is simply trying to find a group where he can lose his fears. He is simply seeking company. He cannot be alone, he is afraid to be alone. He cannot trust himself. A follower is never ready for insecurity; he comes to a guru, to a master, to seek protection, shelter, to hide behind him. He is seeking a father figure.

Freedom

Freedom is maturity; licence is very childish. Freedom is possible only when you are so integrated that you can take the responsibility of being free. The world is not free because people are not mature. Revolutionaries have been doing many things down the centuries, but everything fails. Utopians have been continuously thinking of how to free mankind, but nobody bothers, because man cannot be free unless he is integrated. Only a Buddha can be free, a Mahavira can be free, a Christ, a Mohammed can be free, a Zarathustra can be free, because freedom means being aware. If you are not aware then the state is needed, the government is needed, the police is needed, the court is needed. Then freedom has to be cut from everywhere. Then freedom exists only in name; in fact it doesn't exist. How can freedom exist when governments exist? It is impossible. But what to do?

Friendliness

Friendliness is a quality, not a relationship. It has nothing to do with anybody else, it is basically an inner quality. You can be friendly even when you are alone. You cannot be in a friendship when you are alone – another is needed – but friendliness is a kind of fragrance. A flower opens in the jungle and even if nobody passes by it is still fragrant. It does not matter whether anybody comes to know of it or not, it is its quality. Nobody may ever know about it, but that does not matter; it is rejoicing.

Friendship can exist only between one person and another person or at the most between a person and an animal – a horse, a dog. But friendliness can exist even with a rock, with a river, with a mountain, with a cloud, with a faraway star. Friendliness is unlimited because it is not dependent on another; it is absolutely your own flowering.

Frustration

Frustration comes as a shadow of success. In the poor countries of the East there is no frustration because there is no success, so the shadow is missing. In the rich countries of the West there is great frustration because success has come, all that anyone has ever needed is available and there is no contentment. Success has failed – that's the frustration ...

In the West, because of frustration, people are becoming more and more interested in meditation, prayer, contemplation. That is part of the same frustration.

My own observation is that a person becomes a meditator only when there are only two possibilities: suicide or transformation. Only at that point, at that peak of frustration, does one turn in. The turning in cannot happen in a lukewarm person; it happens only when things are really hot and you have been frustrated totally by the outside world and all exterior journeys, all extroversion seems meaningless, all ways have proved false. Only then does the desire, the longing for an inner pilgrimage open up.

Future

We are always thinking in terms of the future. Stop thinking in terms of the future; that is the way to prolong the life of the mind, to nourish it. The future is the food of the mind. The moment you become decisive about the present, the mind has started dying. It is the beginning of the end, the end of the mind. And the end of the mind is the beginning of your real existence, your real life.

Gambler

Find out why you are feeling bored. Change.

Life is short. Take risks, be a gambler. What can you lose?

We come with empty hands, we go with empty hands. There is nothing to lose. Just a little time to be playful, to sing a beautiful song.

Each moment is so precious.

Gnostic

This word is beautiful. 'Gnostic' means one who knows; 'gnosis' means knowledge. 'Agnostic' means one who knows not; agnostic means one who knows only one thing, that he knows not. Be an agnostic. That is the beginning of real religion.

Don't believe, don't disbelieve. Don't be a Hindu, don't be a Jain, don't be a Christian, otherwise you will go on groping in darkness forever and ever. Unless you drop all ideologies, all philosophies, all religions, all systems of thought, and go inside empty, with nothing in your hand, with no idea ... How can you have an idea of God? You have not known him. Just go within, with a great desire to know, but with no idea of knowledge. Go with an intense longing to know, with a passionate love to know what is there, but don't carry any ideas given to you by others.

Drop them outside. That is the greatest barrier for the seeker on the path of truth.

God

All religions think everything has had to be created, otherwise where has it come from? But they don't think, 'Where does God come from?' If God created the world, who created him? And if God can be uncreated, then what is the point of bringing in an unnecessary hypothesis?

This is a basic principle of all scientific research: don't bring in unnecessary hypotheses. Work it out with the minimum of hypotheses. If God is to be created by another, bigger God, you will end in an absurdity, what logicians call *regressum infinitum*. You will regress into infinity and you will not find the answer. The question will remain exactly where it was: who created the last God?

Existence is enough. Hence I teach godliness, but not God. God is the invention of the priest. God is a fiction to console you, to make you afraid, to make you guilty. All religions depend on your guilt, on your fear – but that is not authentic religiousness. Authentic religiousness will make you unafraid, fearless – not a slave, not a puppet in the hands of some unknown God, some fiction.

Godliness

There is no God but godliness. It is a quality, a fragrance. You experience it, you don't see it. And when you experience it, it is not something out there as an object; it is something *in here*, in your heart of hearts. It is your subjectivity, it is your consciousness.

So there is no question of belief and there is no question of seeing either.

There is godliness, but there is no God. Whenever I use the word 'God' I simply mean godliness. Remember it. Translate it always as 'godliness'. There is a quality of godliness, but there is no God.

But people want a God, not godliness; they are not interested in godliness. That's why people like Buddha could not have much influence. Buddha and his whole religion disappeared from India, where Buddha was born, and one of the most fundamental reasons for it was that he emphasized godliness and not God.

You have to grow into godliness; it is not something ready-made that you can possess. It is not something that you can pray to, it is not something that you can ask anything of. It is not already there, it has to be created in the innermost core of your being. It is like love – it has to bloom in you, you have to release its fragrance. You have to become godly. Only then is there God; otherwise there is no God.

Growth

Growth is not soft; growth is painful.

All growth is towards the unknown, towards the soft, towards the fragile, towards the indefinable. Growth is a by-product of the enquiry into truth.

If you want to grow, drop the past. The past is no more, it is absolutely irrelevant, but it goes on interfering. You go on judging according to it; you go on saying, 'This is right and that is wrong,' and all those ideas of right and wrong, all those judgements are coming from something which is dead. Your dead past remains so heavy on you that it does not allow you to move. Drop the past completely.

The second thing to remember is not to create expectations for the future. Things are not going to happen

according to you, things are going to happen according to
the whole. The wave, the small wave in the ocean, cannot
be the deciding factor. The ocean decides; the wave has to
go along with it. If the wave wants to go to the east, but the
winds are not going to the east, if the ocean is not willing,
then the wave will suffer. It will call it fate, circumstances,
social conditions, the economic structure, the capitalist
society, the bourgeois culture, the Freudian unconscious
… and even growing pains. But that is just shifting the
responsibility. The real thing is that you are suffering from
your expectations.

The ultimate growth is simply to say 'yes' – to say 'yes'
with as much joy as a child says 'no'. That is a second childhood. And the man who can say 'yes' with tremendous
freedom and joy, with no hesitation, with no strings
attached, with no conditions, a pure and simple joy, a pure
and simple 'yes', that man has become a sage. That man
lives in harmony. And his harmony is of a totally different
dimension than the harmony of trees, animals and birds.
They live in harmony because they cannot say 'no' and the
sage lives in harmony because he does not say 'no'.
Between the two, the birds and the Buddhas, are the
human beings – immature, childish, stuck somewhere, still
trying to say 'no', to have some sense of freedom.

So learn to say 'no' when it is time to say 'no', but don't
get stuck with it. Slowly, slowly, see that there is a higher
freedom that comes with 'yes', and a greater harmony.

Guidance

All the teachers of the world have been imposing their own
ideas, their images on people who are searching and
seeking guidance. It is one of the most dangerous games to

play, because you are always the loser. If a teacher succeeds in imposing certain directions, certain patterns and disciplines, according to me it is not guidance, it is misguidance. Because nobody knows your unique self – only you can know it. And you have to grow according to your nature, not according to anybody's guidance.

To be natural, to be spontaneous, is enough. All guides have been 'misguides'. The whole of humanity is tremendously misguided. You can see it. Otherwise why would there be so much insanity? Why there would be so much misery, so much agony and spiritual suffering? The reason is that nobody has been allowed to be their natural selves.

All 'shoulds' and all 'should nots' have to be abandoned. You simply have to listen to your own inner voice and go wherever it leads. Just go without bothering whether people think it is right or wrong.

If you can do this, if you can become just your own self, if you can blossom into your intrinsic nature, then you will have blissfulness – a peace which cannot be expressed in words – and a certain poetry to your being, a certain dance to your being, because you will be in tune with existence. To be in tune with yourself is the only way to be in tune with existence. Nobody needs personal guidance, because all personal guidance is a beautiful name for dependence on somebody who is going to distort you.

I don't offer any guidance – I don't tell you you should be this or that. I simply say you should become silent, so that you can listen to your still, small voice. That is your real guide; the guide is within you.

Guilt

Guilt is the trade secret of all the so-called established religions. That's their way: create guilt in people, make them feel bad about themselves. Don't let them be respectful of their own lives; let them feel condemned. Let them feel, deep down, that they are ugly, that they are not of any worth, that they are dust, and then of course they will be ready to be guided by any fool. They will be more than ready to become dependent, in the hope that somebody will lead them to the ultimate light.

These are the people who have been exploiting you for centuries.

Gurus

Gurus and disciples are mind phenomena. Because your mind needs gurus, there are gurus. You create them. Because you want to be taught, there are teachers. You need them. This is a game. Some people enjoy it, so they play it. If you enjoy it, play it deeply; if you don't enjoy it, forget it.

The word 'guru' has become almost condemnatory, yet the root meaning of the word is beautiful. The word originally means 'one who is more consolidated, crystallized, one who has more weight'. In Hindi, gravitational force is called *guruthwa karshan*. Just as the Earth pulls things to itself with gravitational force, so people gravitate toward the guru without his doing anything. The Earth is not doing anything while pulling you; it is just the nature of the Earth that anything that is within its gravitational field will start being pulled towards it.

So 'guru' means one who has weight, who is centred, rooted, and has a gravitational force. But that original

 *The ABC of Enlightenment*

meaning has been lost. 'Guru' has become almost a dirty word, particularly since Indian gurus started appearing in the West. And it has to be so, because the people who came to the West were not gurus at all. They came to the West to exploit people. They were knowledgeable about many things of which the West was unaware. They were more philosophical, more theological, more argumentative. That has been a professional thing in India for centuries. So when they came to the West they immediately had a great impact. The Christian minister looked very poor; even the most scholarly rabbi was no competition.

And those who came were not very great men. They came to the West to have a following, to collect money and finally to take that money to India to build temples and places for them and their disciples to live in. But it was all a materialistic thing; there was nothing of the spirit in it at all. So naturally 'guru' became a tainted word.

Happiness

Always find something to be happy about. Life is short and happiness is very difficult, so don't miss an opportunity to be happy. Ordinarily we go on doing the opposite: we don't miss an opportunity to be unhappy.

To be happy is a great talent. Great intelligence, great awareness, almost genius is needed to be happy. To be unhappy is nothing. Even stupid people are unhappy.

It is very easy to be unhappy because the whole mind lives through unhappiness. If you remain happy for a long time, the mind starts disappearing, because there is no connection between happiness and the mind. Happiness is of the beyond.

Harmony

God is the harmony of all that is, and everything is harmonious. The trees are swaying with the wind; there is harmony. They are not fighting the wind, they are dancing with the wind. The stars are moving in tremendous harmony. This vast existence is a great orchestra: everything is in tune with everything else. There is no conflict, no division, no disharmony.

Only human beings can believe that we are separate, because we have consciousness and consciousness gives you the alternative. You can either think yourself separate – then you fall into misery and hell – or you can try to understand the unity of life – and then suddenly there is bliss. To be one with the whole is bliss; to be separate from the whole is misery.

Healing

The word 'healing' comes from the same root as the word 'whole'. 'Whole', 'health', 'healing' and 'holy' all come from the same root. To be healed means to be joined with the whole. To be ill means to be disconnected from the whole. An ill person is one who has simply developed blocks between himself and the whole, so something is disconnected. The function of the healer is to reconnect it.

When somebody is ill, he has lost the capacity to heal himself. He is no longer aware of his own healing source. The healer has to help him to reconnect. The healer is in relationship with the whole, so he can become a connector, a link between the ill person and his healing source. The patient who is no longer directly connected with the source becomes indirectly connected. And once the energy starts flowing, he is healed.

Health

Whenever you are healthy you don't know anything about your body – you forget it. Whenever you have an illness, you cannot forget your body. When you have a headache you cannot forget your head. When you don't have a headache, where is your head? You forget about it completely. Whatever is healthy is forgotten, but whatever is ill is remembered – it becomes a continuous note in the mind, a continuous tension in the mind.

And the ego is an illness, a substantial illness, because you continuously have to remember that you are somebody. This shows that you are in a deep 'dis-ease'. Disease creates the ego; a perfectly healthy, natural being forgets about himself completely. He is like a cloud, like a breeze, like a rock, like a tree, like a bird, but never like a man. He is not like a man because only illness, like a wound, has to be remembered.

Remembering is a safety mechanism: if there is a thorn in your foot, you have to remember it. The mind will return to the spot again and again because the thorn has to be taken out. If you forget it, the thorn will remain there and it will become dangerous; it may poison the whole body. When you have a headache, your body is telling you to take note of it, because something has to be done. If you forget it, the headache may become dangerous.

So the body tells you whenever there is something wrong – it attracts your attention. But when the body is healthy, you forget it. The same applies to the mind. When your consciousness is healthy, there is no ego – you don't know anything about yourself. You don't go on reminding yourself 'I am this or that', you simply relax. You are, but there is no 'I'. It is a simple *am*-ness, an *is*-ness, but there is no 'I', no crystallized ego. The self is not there.

Heart

Free the energy from your head – it is imprisoned there – and allow it to move into the heart, and then into the being, which is your real centre. The heart is midway between the head and the being. Thinking is head; it creates questions and never gives you any answers. It is the world of philosophy, the world of the fools. Below it is the world of feeling, heart; it is the world of the poets.

Have you observed the fact that philosophers ask, poets answer? All poetry is an answer, no poetry is a question. No poetry has a question mark on it; it is an answer. The heart answers! Hence it is far better to come into the world of feeling; that is wiser.

But still you are a little way away from absolutely clear insight, because when the insight is clear there is not even an answer, let alone a question. The philosopher questions, the poet answers, and the mystic is neither interested in questioning nor interested in answering. If you come to a mystic, his whole work is to destroy your questions, your answers, everything that you are carrying along with you, to make you utterly empty. That is the moment when insight starts functioning and you become innocent.

Heaven and Hell

Heaven and hell are not geographical. If you go in search of them you won't find them anywhere in the world. They are within you, they are psychological. The mind is heaven, the mind is hell; the mind has the capacity to become either. But we go on looking for everything outside because to go inside is very difficult. We are outgoing. If somebody says there is a God, we look at the sky. Somewhere, sitting there, will be the divine person.

When you are psychically attuned with existence, when you are silent, you are in heaven. When you are disturbed, when you lose your silence, when you are distracted and there are ripples and ripples in the lake of your consciousness and all the mirror-like quality of consciousness is lost, you are in hell.

Hell simply means disharmony within you – and within existence too. The moment you are harmonious within yourself and within existence – and they are two sides of the same coin – you are immediately in heaven.

Home

Everybody has a deep longing for home but it has nothing to do with the physical home, though the physical home has become an excuse for it. We don't know our real home so we create a small home and we cling to it. To convert a house into a home is a psychological trick – it helps, it is like a tranquilizer. It is like a favourite blanket to a small child. It helps us to feel secure, to feel that we are not uprooted, that we have roots, that we have somewhere to go, that we belong somewhere. Hence we create countries, nations, motherlands, fatherlands, churches, temples and a thousand and one things, but the search is always for home.

In fact, we don't have any home on this Earth. Your home is not outside yourself, it is somewhere inside, very deep in the innermost core of your being, but to go there is a long journey and arduous and dangerous.

Hope

Hopeless people hope. Blind people think sooner or later they will attain to eyes. In the dark night of your souls you cling to the hope that there must be a dawn. To tolerate the present misery you have to create an optimistic attitude so that you can hope for a beautiful tomorrow, although it never comes. But in hoping, you can tolerate. At least you can dilute your misery a little bit, you can avoid being too disturbed by it. You can remain occupied. You can close your eyes to your anguish.

Humour

To me, humour is the most sacred experience in life. And it can be proven: no animal except man has a sense of humour. Can you expect a buffalo to laugh? Can you expect a donkey to have a sense of humour? The moment your saints become serious, they fall into the category of buffaloes and donkeys: they are no longer human, because humour is the only special quality that human consciousness has. This shows that only at a certain point of evolution does humour manifest itself.

And the higher you go, the more playful will be your approach to life and its problems. They will no longer be burdens, it will be a joy to solve them. Life will not be a sin – it is serious people who have made life a sin – life will be a reward, a gift. Those who are wasting life in seriousness are being ungrateful to existence.

Learn to laugh with the flowers and the stars and you will feel a strange weightlessness coming into your being, as if you have grown wings and can fly.

Immortality

The secret of immortality is not such a secret that it cannot be discovered. In fact it is an open secret.

Just a little bit of digging inside yourself and you can discover it. Just a few layers of garbage have to be removed. We call that garbage 'the mind'. Thoughts and desires and memories are crowding inside the mind and because of the crowd we cannot see our own truth. Once we are able to create a little gap, a little space, the truth can be discovered.

The truth is that we are immortal. The truth is that we were never born and we will never die, that birth and death are episodes in our eternal life. Thousands of times we have taken birth and thousands of times we have left the body. It is because of the mind that we go on coming back again and again. It is because of the mind that the wheel of birth and death goes on turning.

If we drop out of the mind, the wheel stops. And that's the whole art of meditation: how to drop out of the mind and how to enter the space called no-mind.

Imperfection

Perfectionism is the root cause of all neurosis. Nobody can be perfect – nobody *need* be perfect. Life is beautiful because everything is imperfect. Perfection is death; imperfection is life. It is because of imperfection that growth is possible. If you are perfect then there is no growth, no movement. Then nothing can happen to you; everything has already happened. You will be utterly dead.

Individuality

You may not be aware that the word 'personality' comes from the Greek. It means 'a mask'. In Greek drama, in the ancient days, every actor used to have a mask. *Persona* means 'mask', and from *persona* has come the word 'personality'. Unless you drop your personality you will not be able to find your individuality.

Individuality is given by existence; personality is imposed by society. Personality is a social convenience. Society cannot tolerate individuality, because individuality will not follow like a sheep. Individuality has the quality of the lion; the lion moves alone.

Sheep are always in a crowd, hoping that being in the crowd will feel cosy. Being in a crowd you feel more protected, secure. If somebody attacks, there is every possibility of saving yourself in a crowd, but alone? Only the lions move alone.

And every one of you is born a lion, but society goes on conditioning you, programming your mind to be a sheep. It gives you a personality, a cosy personality – very nice, very convenient, very obedient. But it is not individuality.

Insight

All the great scientists say that whenever they discovered something, they discovered it not by thinking but when the thinking had stopped and there was an interval, a gap.

Into that gap came the insight – the intuitive flash, like lightning.

When thought stops, your thinking is pure. It looks paradoxical, so let me repeat, when thought stops, your thinking is pure, your capacity to reflect reality is pure.

Inspiration

The word 'inspiration' is dangerous. First it is inspiration, then it becomes following, then it becomes imitation and you end up being a carbon copy. There is no need to be inspired by anybody. Not only is there no need, it is dangerous.

Each individual is unique. Nobody can follow anybody else. Inspiration has been a curse, not a blessing. Learn from every source, enjoy every unique being that you come across, but never follow anybody and never try to become exactly like somebody else. You can only be yourself.

It is a strange phenomenon that the people who have become an inspiration for millions of other people were themselves never inspired by anybody – but nobody takes note of this fact. Gautama Buddha was never inspired by anybody, and that's what made him a great source of inspiration. Socrates was not inspired by anybody, and that's what makes him so unique. All these people whom you think of as sources of inspiration were never inspired by anybody else. Yes, they learned, they tried to understand all kinds of people, they loved unique individuals, but they did not follow anybody. They tried to be themselves.

Intellect

Intellect is of the mind: it depends on memory, it functions through borrowed knowledge. All our educational systems are rooted in intellectual development, hence they all depend on memory. The examinations in our schools, colleges and universities are not examining intelligence, they are only testing how good a memory you have. But memory is not an indication of intelligence. Memory is mechanical. A computer can have a better memory than a man of genius, but a computer has no intelligence.

The human mind is nothing but a bio-computer, one that has evolved over a long, long time. And intelligence is when the memory is silent and the intellect is not functioning, when the whole mind is at rest.

Intelligence is something beyond mind.

In English there is a problem because the same word is used for both and they are totally different. In Sanskrit, and in all Eastern languages, we have different names for each: intellect is called *bodhi,* the faculty of knowledge; and intelligence is called *pragya,* the faculty of knowing, not knowledge.

Knowledge is always dead; it is information. And all our educational systems are doing with students exactly what we are doing with computers – feeding them with more and more information. But no computer can answer a question for which it has not been programmed. Intellect can only answer that which it already knows; it is stale, it belongs to yesterday.

Intelligence is a response to a new situation, a response not from your past memories but from your present awareness. You don't function as a computer, you don't search for the answer in your memory, rather you simply open your consciousness to the situation and allow the spontaneous response to arise.

In other words, intelligence is spontaneous responsibility.

Intelligence

Intelligence simply means the ability to respond, because life is a flux. You have to be aware and to see what is demanded of you, what the challenge is in each situation. The intelligent person behaves according to the situation and the stupid person behaves according to the ready-made answers. Whether they come from Buddha, Christ or Krishna, it does not matter, the stupid person always carries scriptures around; he is afraid to depend on himself. The intelligent person depends on his own insight; he trusts his own being. He loves and respects himself. The unintelligent person respects others.

Jealousy

Jealousy is comparison. And we have been taught to compare, we have been conditioned to compare. Somebody else has a better house, somebody else has a more beautiful body, somebody else has more money, somebody else has a more charismatic personality. Compare, always compare, go on comparing yourself with everybody else and great jealousy will be the outcome; it is the by-product of the conditioning for comparison.

It is good that you don't compare yourself with trees, otherwise you will start feeling very jealous: why aren't you green? It is better not to compare yourself with birds, with rivers, with mountains, otherwise you will suffer.

If you drop the comparisons, jealousy disappears. Then you simply know you are you, and you are nobody else, and there is no need to be anybody else.

Comparison is a very foolish attitude, because each person is unique and incomparable. Once this understanding settles in you, jealousy disappears. You are just yourself: nobody has ever been like you and nobody will ever be like you. And you need not be like anybody else either.

Joy

Joy is a subtle harmony. When your body, your mind and your heart are functioning together in deep accord, joy arises. In joy something is contributed by the body and something is contributed by the mind, but the major part is contributed by the heart.

Joy is far superior to pleasure, to happiness. It is far more delicate, softer, more flowerlike. If one has to choose between the three, then one should choose joy. Joy contains something of pleasure, something of happiness and something more.

Judgement Day

There is no God, so don't be afraid of Judgement Day. There is never going to be any Judgement Day. And anyway, just think, even if your God is absolutely powerful, how many millions of people, all the people who have lived over the millennia, will be gathered on one day in one court? And half of them will be women, who won't care about the court or anything; they will go yakketty-yak, yakketty-yak … There will be an immeasurable crowd shouting for judgement. I don't think it will be possible just in 24 hours to decide who is going where.

Judgement Day – the very idea is stupid. There will be so many files on everybody that it will take eternity for God to sort out the files.

Justice

Mullah Nasruddin is chosen to be an honorary magistrate. The first case appears. He hears one side and declares to the court, 'Within five minutes I will be back with the judgement.'

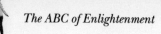

The court clerk cannot believe it – he has not heard the other side! He whispers in his ear, 'What are you doing? You have heard only one party, one side. The other side is waiting, and without hearing them you cannot give any judgement.'

Mullah Nasruddin says, 'Don't try to confuse me. Just now I am absolutely clear. If I hear the other side too, then there is bound to be confusion.'

Karma

Certainly each action has its result, but not somewhere far away in a future life. The action and the result are continuous, they are part of one process. Do you think sowing the seed and reaping the crop are separate? It is one process. What begins with sowing the seed one day becomes thousands of seeds. That's what you call your crop. It is the same seed which has exploded into thousands of seeds. No death intervenes, no afterlife is needed; it is a continuum.

So the thing to remember is that yes, every action is bound to have consequences, but they will not be somewhere else, you will have them here and now. Most likely you will get them almost instantly.

When you are kind to someone, don't you feel a certain joy? A certain peace? A certain meaningfulness? Don't you feel contented with what you have done? Have you ever felt that contentment when you are boiling with anger, when you have hurt somebody, when you are mad with rage? Have you ever felt a peace, a silence descending on you then? No, it is impossible. You will certainly feel something, but it will be sadness that you acted like a fool again, that you did that stupid thing that you said you would never do again.

Knowledge

Knowledge has its uses, it is not absolutely useless. But if you are going inwards it becomes more and more useless, and the deeper you go, the more useless it is. If you are going outwards, the farther you go out into the world, the more useful it becomes. The world respects the knowledgeable person. It needs experts; it needs all kinds of people with information, knowledge, expertise. But in the inner world the question does not arise; in the inner world knowledge becomes a hindrance. That which is useful in the outside world becomes a barrier to the inner. Knowledge is a bridge to the world, but it is a barrier to inner exploration.

Knowledge tries to control. Knowledge makes you powerful. Ignorance makes you humble. So remember not to become knowledgeable. Never allow knowledge to collect around you. Every day, knowledge is accumulated through experience; every day, throw it away. It is dust that gathers on the mirror of consciousness.

Koan

A koan is a puzzle that has no solution. It is never solved, but as you go on meditating and becoming silent and silent and more silent, it dissolves. Suddenly there is no puzzle, no problem, nothing to solve. The koan is a thought and it disappears in deep meditation along with all other thoughts. Zen has thousands of koans.

Kundalini

Existence is energy, the movement of energy in so many ways and so many forms. As far as human existence is concerned, this energy is kundalini energy. Kundalini is the focused energy of the human body and human psyche.

Energy can be either manifested or unmanifested. It can remain in the seed or it can sprout in a manifested form. All energy is either in the seed or in the manifested form. Kundalini means your total potential. But it is a seed; it is possibility. The ways to awaken kundalini are ways to make your potential actual.

So first of all, kundalini is not something unique. It is only human energy as such. But ordinarily only a part of it is functioning, a very minute part. Even that part is not functioning harmoniously; it is in conflict. That is the misery, the anguish. If your energy can function harmoniously then you feel bliss, but if it is in conflict, if it is antagonistic to itself, then you feel miserable. All misery means that your energy is in conflict, and all happiness, all bliss, means that your energy is in harmony.

Laughter

Laughter is the only thing that is special to human beings –
not reason, but laughter. Animals can also reason – they
reason in their own way. But they cannot joke, they cannot
laugh, they cannot see the funny side; that is impossible for
them. All animals are serious people and all serious people
are animals! The moment you get rid of your seriousness
you get rid of your animal nature.

Complete laughter is a rare phenomenon. When each
cell of your body laughs, when each fibre of your being
pulsates with joy, then it brings great relaxation. There are
a few activities which are immensely valuable; laughter is
one of those activities. Singing and dancing are also of the
same quality, but laughter is the quickest.

Laughter is life, is love, is light. Laughter in its purest form
is a dance of all your energies. In really deep laughter the
mind disappears. Laughter is not a part of the mind or of the
heart. When real laughter happens – belly laughter, as it is
called – then it comes from your very core. Ripples start
spreading from your very centre towards your circumference.
Just as when you throw a rock into a silent lake and ripples
arise, so real laughter arises from your centre and moves
towards your circumference. It is almost like an earthquake!
Every single cell of your body, every fibre, dances in tune.

Laziness

If the whole world becomes lazy, we will have such a beautiful world with no wars, no atomic weapons, no nuclear weapons, no crime, no jails, no judges, no policemen, no presidents, no prime ministers. People will be so lazy that they won't need all this nonsense.

Just think about it some time: has any lazy person in the world ever done anything wrong? And still poor lazy people are condemned.

Lazy people have never done any harm to anybody – they cannot. They will not go to that much trouble. It is the active people who are the real problem.

Lies

We live in lies. We talk about the truth but we live in lies. In fact, talking about the truth is just a camouflage to hide the lies of life. And we have become so accustomed to it, so skilful at it that we are not even aware of those lies. We go on playing those games absolutely unconsciously. It is not even deliberate, it has become a habit.

Start watching when you are lying – and stop it immediately! You will be surprised to discover that you are lying the whole day, sometimes for one reason or another, but more often for no reason at all! It has just become your natural way of behaving. Somebody comes and you smile. The smile is a lie – polite, formal, but still a lie. You say something to somebody – maybe it is just etiquette, but it is a lie all the same. Slowly, slowly, drop all those things and you will see a great transformation. Because the energy that is involved in the lies will be released and only that energy can become truth.

Life

I say to you, life is the only truth there is. There is no other God but life. So allow yourself to be possessed by life in all its forms, colours, dimensions – the whole rainbow, all the notes of the musical scale. It is simple, it is only a question of letting go. Don't push the river, let the river take you to the ocean. It is already on the way there.

Relax, don't be tense and don't try to be spiritual. Don't create any division between matter and spirit. Matter and spirit are simply two sides of the same coin. Relax, rest and go with the river. Be a gambler, not a businessman, and you will know more of God, because the gambler can take risks. The gambler can put all that he has at stake. But the thrill of the gambler when he stakes everything and waits … what is going to happen now? In that very moment a window can open. That very moment can become a transformation of the inner gestalt.

Be a drunkard – be drunk with life, with the wine of existence. Don't remain sober. The sober person remains dead. Drink the wine of life. It has so much poetry and so much love and so much juice.

Logic

Logic believes in two categories: the known and the unknown. That which is unknown today will become known tomorrow. That which is known today was unknown yesterday. So there is not much difference between the known and the unknown; they belong to the same category. Logic does not believe in the unknowable – and the unknowable is the very heart of life, the very heartbeat of the universe.

I am not against logic. Use it – it is a beautiful strategy as far as the marketplace is concerned, the superficial world is concerned – but beware that you don't go on carrying it into deeper layers of life and experience. There it is a hindrance. Logic uses the mind and the mind is helpful in understanding the objective world, but it is a hindrance in understanding the subjective world, because the subjective world is beyond the mind, behind the mind. You can use your eyes to see others, but you cannot use your eyes to see yourself. If you want to see yourself through your own eyes you have to use a mirror. To look in a mirror means you are creating a reflection of yourself, which is not you, certainly not you, but you can see the reflection. Logic can see only the reflected glory of existence; it cannot see existence itself because existence is far deeper than logical formulations.

Loneliness

Once you understand the beauty of your loneliness it becomes aloneness. Then it is no longer empty, then it is no longer nothingness. Then it has a purity – it is so pure that it is formless.

Always remember the difference between aloneness and loneliness. Loneliness is like a wound. Loneliness means you are missing another person. Loneliness means you are thinking of another person constantly, you are hankering for another person constantly. The other is in your fantasy, in your mind, in your dreams. The other is not real, it is imaginary, but it is there and because it is not real you feel lonely.

When you start feeling your aloneness, the other drops from your mind completely. It doesn't shadow your dreams any more, it doesn't touch your purity any more. You are happy with yourself, you are ecstatic with yourself, you are enjoying yourself. Now for the first time you are in tune with your being and with your non-being. You are whole.

Now you can be in love. Now love can flow. But now love will be a sharing, not an escape. Now you can go and share your being – and your non-being also. Now you can share your wholeness. Now you can allow anybody who is open to join your openness, now you can become partners in the eternal journey. This love will not be possessive, because you are ready to be alone anytime. In fact you are happy being alone and you are happy being together – you don't have to choose between the two. Both are good. Whatever the case, you feel happy. Your happiness cannot be destroyed now; another can enjoy it and share it but cannot destroy it.

Lotus

The lotus is one of the most miraculous phenomena in existence, hence in the East it has become the symbol of spiritual transformation. Buddha is seated on a lotus, Vishnu is standing on a lotus. Why a lotus? Because the lotus has one very symbolic significance: it grows out of dirty mud. It is a transformation symbol, it is a metamorphosis. The mud is dirty, maybe stinking; the lotus is fragrant, and it has come out of the stinking mud.

Love

Love should not be in any way possessive. It should not be exclusive, it should be inclusive. Only when love is inclusive will you know what it is. When love is exclusive, exclusive to one person, you are narrowing it down so much that you will kill it. You are destroying its infinity. You are trying to put the whole sky into a small space which cannot contain it.

One should be in love. Love should not be just a relationship, it should be a state of being. And whenever you love one, through the one you love the all. And if love has *really* happened you will suddenly find that you have started loving trees and birds and the sky and people. When you have fallen in love with one person, what exactly has happened? When you fall in love with one woman you have fallen in love with all women. The one woman is just a representative, the one woman is just an example of all the women that have existed in the world, that are existing in the world and that will exist in the world. That one woman is just a door to womanhood. But the woman is not only a woman, she is a human being too. So you have fallen in love with all human beings. And the woman is not only a human being, she is a being too. So you have fallen in love with all beings. Once you fall in love you will be surprised that your love energy is released to all. That is true love.

Possessive love is not true love. It is so tiny it suffocates itself and it suffocates the other person too. But this has been the case up to now – love has never been inclusive. You have been taught exclusive love. But love can be inclusive. You can love the whole world.

Loyalty

In place of love and trust, we have created a false value: loyalty. The loyal person is only superficially concerned with love. He goes through all the gestures of love, but he means nothing by them; his heart stays out of his formal gestures.

A slave is loyal, but do you think anybody who is a slave, whose pride and dignity have been taken away, can love the person who has harmed him so deeply? He will hate him, and if the chance arises, he may kill him. But on the surface, he will remain loyal – he has to. But it is not out of joy, it is out of fear. It is not out of love, it is out of a conditioned mind that says that you have to be loyal to your master. It is the loyalty of the dog to his master.

Lust

Lust means sex is the focus, the centre of things. You don't have any sense of beauty, you don't have any aesthetic sense. Can you think of a man with any aesthetic sense going to a prostitute? Impossible. Can you think of a man with any aesthetic sense raping a woman? Impossible. Or even hitting a woman in the crowd or just touching her body in such a way as if he was not meaning to touch her, as if it happened accidentally? That is not love, that is not sensibility, that is not sensitivity. It is lust.

Lust means you don't respect the other person at all. You have a deep, repressed desire, repressed sexuality, which comes out in many perverted ways. Then your eyes become covered and coloured only with sexuality.

Luxury

I would like the whole Earth to live in luxury. Certainly, I know that today that is not the case. Many people are not even getting the minimum necessities of life. But I am not going to torture myself just because of that, because that is not going to help them.

Once a country becomes rich, it becomes sensitive. Once a country becomes rich, affluent, it becomes aware of many, many dimensions of life that have always been there but no one had time to look. People of the rich country start looking at music, painting, poetry and ultimately meditation – because meditation is the last luxury. There is no greater luxury than meditation.

Mantras

Chanting a mantra can only dull your mind; all repetition dulls the mind, makes you silly and stupid. If you simply go on chanting a mantra, it kills your sensitivity, it creates boredom, it brings a sort of slumber to your consciousness. You become more unconscious than conscious, you start slipping into sleep. Mothers have known always that when a child is restless and cannot go to sleep they must sing a lullaby. A lullaby is a mantra. The mother repeats something again and again and again and the child feels bored. The constant repetition creates a monotonous atmosphere. The child cannot escape anywhere – the mother is sitting by the side of the bed and repeating the lullaby. The child cannot escape; the child cannot say, 'Shut up!' He has to listen. The only escape available is to go into sleep, so he tries that – to avoid this lullaby and to avoid this mother! A mantra works in the same way: you start repeating a certain word and then you create a monotonous state for yourself. All monotony is deadening; all monotony dulls you, destroys your sharpness.

In the old monasteries all over the world – Christian, Hindu, Buddhist – in all the monasteries they have tried the same trick on a bigger scale. The life of a monastery is routine, absolutely fixed. Each morning you have to get up at three o'clock or five o'clock, and then the same daily round starts. You have to do the same activities the whole day for your whole life. This is spreading a mantra over your whole life, creating a routine.

By and by, doing the same thing again and again, a person becomes more like a somnambulist. Whether he is awake or asleep makes no difference, he simply goes on making the empty gestures and empty movements. He loses all distinction between sleeping and waking.

You can go to the old monasteries and watch monks walking in their sleep. They have become robots. Between when they get up in the morning and when they go to sleep, there is no distinction – the territories overlap. And it is exactly the same every day. In fact, the word 'monotonous' and the word 'monastery' come from the same root.

You can create such a monotonous life that intelligence is not needed. When intelligence is not needed you become dull, and when you become dull, of course you start feeling a certain sort of peace, a certain silence, but it is not real, it is pseudo.

Real silence is very alive, throbbing. Real silence is positive; it has energy in it, it is intelligent, aware, full of life and zest. It has enthusiasm in it.

Marriage

Marriage is a great teaching; it is an opportunity to learn something – to learn that dependence is not love, that to depend means conflict, anger, rage, hatred, jealousy, possessiveness, domination. You have to learn not to depend. But for that you will need great meditativeness so that you can be so blissful on your own that you don't need another person. When you don't need another, dependence disappears.

Once you don't need another, you can share your joy – and sharing is beautiful.

I would like a different kind of relating in the world. I call it 'relating' just to make it different from your old kind of relationship. I would like a different kind of marriage in the world. I will not call it 'marriage' because that word has become poisoned. I would like to call it just a friendship; no legal bondage, just a loving togetherness. No promise for tomorrow – this moment is enough. And if you love each other this moment, and if you enjoy each other this moment, if you can share with each other this moment, the next moment will be born out of it; it will be enriched. As time passes by, your love will become deeper, it will start having new dimensions, but it will not create any bondage.

Materialism

Never create any antagonism between materialism and spirituality – they go together, just like body and soul. Remain materialistic and use your materialism as a stepping-stone to spirituality.

This idea always creates much confusion in people's minds because they have always been taught that poverty is something spiritual. That is utter nonsense. Poverty is the most unspiritual thing in the world. A poor man cannot be spiritual. He can try, but his spirituality will remain superficial. He has not yet been disillusioned by riches, so how can he be spiritual? A great disillusionment is needed, a great disillusionment with the outer world; then you turn inwards. The turning in comes only at a point when you are utterly disillusioned with the outside – when you have seen the world, you have lived the world and you have come to know that there is nothing in it; it is all soap bubbles, momentary experiences. They promise much but they deliver nothing, and in the end only emptiness is left in your hands.

Maturity

When I say 'maturity', I mean an inner integrity. And this inner integrity comes only when you stop making others responsible, when you stop saying that other people are creating your suffering, when you start realizing that you are the creator of your suffering. This is the first step towards maturity: 'I am responsible. Whatever is happening, it is my doing.'

You feel sad. Is that your doing? You may feel very disturbed by that feeling, but if you can remain with it, sooner or later you will be able to stop doing many things.

This is what the theory of karma is all about. You are responsible. Don't say society is responsible, don't say that parents are responsible, don't say economic conditions are responsible, don't throw the responsibility onto anybody else – *you* are responsible. In the beginning, this will look like a burden because now you cannot throw the responsibility onto anyone else. But take it.

Meditation

Meditation in the East is not what is understood by it in the West. In the West, meditation means contemplation: meditating on God, meditating on truth, meditating on love. But if you meditate *on* something, you are not meditating at all, because you are focusing on something outside yourself. It may be love, it may be truth, it may be God, it makes no difference.

Meditation in the East has a totally different meaning, just the opposite of the Western meaning. Meditation in the East means having no object in the mind, no content in the mind, not meditating upon something but dropping everything – *neti, neti,* neither this nor that. Meditation is emptying yourself of all content. When there is no thought moving inside you there is stillness, and that stillness is meditation. Not even a ripple arises in the lake of your consciousness, and that silent lake, absolutely still, is meditation.

And in that meditation you will know what truth is, you will know what love is, you will know what godliness is. Not by meditating *on* God … See the point: how can you meditate on God? You don't know anything about God. All your meditation is going to be just imagination, an exercise of imagination. You don't know truth – what are you going to meditate upon? Some idea given by others, some belief, some concept? That is not going to help.

First *become* meditation, and then in meditation, truth, godliness, love and all that is transcendental will be revealed to you.

Meditation is just being, not doing anything – no action, no thought, no emotion. It is very simple – a totally relaxed state of consciousness where you are not doing anything. The moment doing enters, you become tense, anxious. What to do? How to do it? How to succeed? How not to fail? You have already moved into the future.

In meditation you just are. And it is a sheer delight. Meditation is just being delighted in your own presence; meditation is a delight in your own being.

Where does this delight come from, when you are not doing anything? It comes from nowhere or it comes from everywhere. It is not caused by anything, because existence itself is made of the stuff called joy. It needs no cause, no reason. If you are unhappy you have a reason to be unhappy; if you are happy, you are simply happy – there is no reason for it. Your mind tries to find a reason because it cannot believe in 'the uncaused' because it cannot control the uncaused – with the uncaused the mind simply becomes impotent. So the mind goes on finding some reason or other. But I would like to tell you that whenever you are happy, you are happy for no reason at all, whenever you are unhappy, you have a reason to be unhappy, because happiness is just the stuff you are made of. It is your very being, it is your innermost core. Joy is your inner most core.

Metaphysics

During a Yiddish play, the curtain fell suddenly and the manager of the theatre stepped out before the audience, in the last degree of agitation.

'Ladies and gentlemen,' he said, 'I'm distressed to have to tell you that the great and beloved actor, Mendel Kalb, has just had a fatal heart attack in his dressing-room and we cannot continue.'

Whereupon a formidable middle-aged woman in the balcony rose and cried out, 'Quick! Give him some chicken soup!'

The manager, surprised, said, 'Madam, I said it was a fatal heart attack. The great Mendel Kalb is dead.'

The woman repeated, 'So quick! Give him some chicken soup.'

The manager again replied, 'Madam! The man is dead! What good will chicken soup do?'

And the woman shouted back, 'What harm?'

Metaphysics – at most, there is one thing that can be said in its favour: it cannot do any harm. It is chicken soup to a dead man. But nothing good comes of it. Nothing can come of it – it is mere words, a mere play of words. So no good can come of it. Of course, no harm either. It is such a futile activity that not even harm comes of it.

Mind

The mind is all that you have experienced, all that you have gone through, all that is already dead – the mind is the dead part of your being. It is the past – the dead hovering over the living. It does not allow you to be here; it does not allow you to be present. It is like a cloud surrounding you: you cannot see through it, your vision is not clear, everything is distorted.

Let this cloud disappear. Let yourself be left with no answers, no conclusions, no philosophies, no religions. Remain open, just open; remain vulnerable, and the truth can happen to you. To be vulnerable is to be intelligent. To know that you don't know is to be intelligent. To know that through the mind you miss reality is to be intelligent. To know that through no-mind the door opens is to be intelligent.

Miracles

Moses parted the ocean … I have been trying to part the water in my bathtub and I have not been able to yet! Those miracles that people have been told about are all inventions. And they have been invented to distract you from the real miracle that can happen to you.

As a result of believing in these fictions, you can forget how to trust reality. Watch what is happening, respect it, trust it and it will deepen, it will become vaster, it will become richer, it will gain many more dimensions – and a real miracle will happen.

And don't refuse to accept the real miracles when they happen, because if you refuse to accept them, then you stop being available to them; then you become closed.

Remain open and vulnerable to the wind and the rain and the sun. Remain available to existence. To me, existence is God and there is no other God. And existence is each moment a miracle – we have just become blind.

Drop your blindness. Become simple and ordinary.

Mistakes

Mistakes are perfectly OK, there is nothing wrong with mistakes. Everybody makes them and everybody has to make them. Don't ask for perfection. Mistakes are good, they keep you human. Otherwise you will either become inhuman or superhuman, and neither is good. To be human is very beautiful, but to remain human one has to err. Why make so much fuss about it?

Don't torture yourself and feel guilty and condemn yourself for making mistakes. There is no need; everybody commits mistakes. Just remember not to commit the same mistake again. Make some new mistakes! That is how you grow. Get fed up with the old mistakes and find new ways to commit new mistakes. Every day make at least one new mistake.

Money

I am not against money, I am against money-mindedness! I am not against possessions, I am against possessiveness. And these are two totally different dimensions, diametrically opposite to each other.

To be against money is stupid. Money is a beautiful means of exchange. Without money there cannot be an evolved culture, society or civilization. Just imagine that money has disappeared from the world. All that is comfortable and convenient would have disappeared with it. People would have been be reduced to utter poverty. Money has done tremendous work; we have to appreciate it. Hence I am not against money, but I am certainly against money-mindedness – and people don't make the distinction.

There is no need to renounce money. Money has to be created, wealth has to be created. Without wealth all science will disappear, all technology will disappear, all the great achievements of man will disappear. Man will not be able to reach the moon, man will not be able to fly. Without money life will become very dumb, just as without language all art, all literature, all poetry, all music will disappear. Just as language helps you to exchange thoughts, to communicate, so money helps you to exchange things; it is also a form of communication.

But money-minded people cling to money; they destroy its whole purpose. Renounce money-mindedness.

Monk

The word 'monk' means one who lives alone, one who escapes from people. And in fact it is relationship that is the opportunity to grow, it is love that is a challenge to growth, it is friendship that brings you to your real flavour. It is life with all its adventures and challenges that helps you to become mature and integrated.

So monks have been taken out of the soil of life. They do not have the opportunity to grow. At most they are like greenhouse plants: bring them into the world and they will immediately shrink and die. They are very fearful people, continuously trembling, afraid of hell, which does not exist, and greedy for heaven, which does not exist – and between hell and heaven missing everything that does exist.

Morality

Moral character simply means something imposed on you by others; it is not really religious. It is a form of domination, a form of slavery, because you have not come to the understanding of what is right and what is wrong; you have been simply told by others. You don't really know whether what you are calling 'moral' is moral or immoral. One thing can be moral in one society and immoral in another society.

Just look around the Earth, expand your vision, and you will be surprised at how many moralities there are. How can this be? Right is right and wrong is wrong! There can't be many moralities. There can't be a Hindu morality or a Mohammedan morality or a Jain morality – but there are. That simply shows that all these moralities are inventions – inventions by different societies to dominate the individuals that make up those societies. Morality is a strategy for imprisoning the individual.

Music

The first musicians, the pioneers, were not really trying to create music, they were trying to find some way to convey the silence, the beauty, the calmness, the soothingness that they felt in meditation. In fact all the arts have their origin in meditation, but music comes the closest because music is nothing but a play between sound and silence.

To the ordinary musician the sound is important. To the master musician the silence is important. He uses sound only to create silence. He raises sound to a high pitch and then drops it so suddenly that you fall into a deep silence.

Mystery
This is the most profound truth, that life in its totality, in its organic wholeness, is absolutely a mystery. It is not a problem that can be solved, it is not a question that can be answered. No amount of knowledge is going to demystify it. It will remain mysterious. Mysteriousness is not something accidental to it. You cannot take it away from it; it is its very soul.

Mysticism
Mysticism is the experience that life is not logic, that life is poetry; that life is not syllogism, that life is a song. Mysticism is the declaration that life can never really be known; it is essentially unknowable.

Science divides existence into two categories: the known and the unknown. The known was unknown one day; it has become known. The unknown is unknown today; tomorrow, or the day after tomorrow, it will also become known. Science believes that sooner or later a point of understanding will arrive when there will be only one category – the known.

Mysticism is the declaration that life consists of three categories: one, the known; another, the unknown; and the third and the most important, the unknowable – that which has not been known and will never be known. And that is the essential core of it all.

Nature

This civilization has failed because it has been against nature. We have tried to be very arrogant with nature; we have been trying to conquer nature, which is utterly ridiculous. We are part of nature! How can we conquer it? We *are* nature; to fight with nature is to fight with ourselves. It is so foolish and so suicidal that later generations will not be able to believe we have committed such a crime.

We have to learn again how to come closer to the trees, to the forest, to the mountains, to the oceans. We have to learn how to befriend them again. We can live joyously only with nature, not against nature. The moment we are against nature, our love energy turns into hatred. If we flow with nature in total harmony, our love grows and matures, becomes more integrated. And the maturing of love is the greatest gift of life.

New Age

The 'new age' movement is just a fashion which will disappear very soon, as all other movements have disappeared. Now you don't see hippies, for example ... All those hippies suddenly disappeared. What happened to their revolution? It was dropping out of society. Why have they dropped back into society? All these movements are very short-lived. They have beautiful names but they don't have a radical philosophy to change human beings.

The new age movement has nothing unique that can transform individuals. It is a fashion, just a passing phase, soon it will die.

I am not part of any movement. What I am doing is something eternal. It has been going on since the first human appeared on the Earth, and it will continue to the last. It is not a movement, it is the very core of evolution.

So don't count me as part of the new age movement. I am not. I am part of the eternal evolution of humankind. The search for truth is neither new nor old. The search for your own being has nothing to do with time; it is non-temporal.

Nirvana

Nirvana is one of the most beautiful words; any language can be proud of this word. It has two meanings, but those two meanings are like two sides of the same coin. One meaning is cessation of the ego and the other meaning is cessation of all desire. It happens simultaneously. The ego and the desire are intrinsically together, they are inseparably together. The moment ego dies, desire disappears, or vice versa: the moment desire is transcended, ego is transcended. And to be without desire, without ego, is to know the ultimate bliss, the eternal ecstasy.

No

Words have their own qualities. You cannot find those qualities in dictionaries. But in real life if you go into the psychology of words, each word has its unique individuality. 'No' gives you power. 'Yes' does not give you power.

Whenever you say 'no', you can feel power; whenever you say 'yes', you can feel love, you can feel compassion, but not power. 'No' is not simply a denial; it is an assertion of power.

No-Mind

If the mind wants to comprehend reality, it will have to go beyond the past and the future. But if it goes beyond the past and the future, it is no longer the mind at all. Hence the insistence of all the great masters of the world that the door to reality is no-mind.

Slip out of the mind and you will know what it is.

Nothingness

Nothingness can either be just emptiness or it can be a tremendous fullness. It can be negative or it can be positive. If it is negative, it is like death, darkness. Religions have called it hell. It is hell because there is no joy in it, no song in it, there is no heartbeat, no dance. Nothing flowers, nothing opens. It is simply empty.

This empty nothingness has created great fear in people. That's why in the West particularly, God has never been called nothingness except by a few mystics like Dionysius, Eckhart, Boehme; but they are not the main current of Western thinking. The West has always conceived nothingness in negative terms, hence it has created a tremendous fear of it. And they go on saying to people that the empty mind is the Devil's workshop.

The East has known the positive aspect of nothingness too; it is one of the greatest contributions to human consciousness. Buddha would laugh at the statement that an empty mind is the Devil's workshop. He would say,

'Only in emptiness, only in nothingness, does godliness happen.' But he would be talking about the positive phenomenon.

Obedience

The whole misery of the world can be explained very simply: every person has been cut, moulded, arranged by others who haven't even bothered to find out what that person was supposed to be by nature. From the very moment the child is born, they start damaging him – all with good intentions, of course. No parent does it consciously, but all parents were conditioned in the same way. They repeat it with their own children because they know nothing else.

The disobedient child is continuously condemned. The obedient child is, on the other hand, continuously praised. But have you heard of any obedient child becoming world-famous in any dimension of creativity? Have you heard of any obedient child winning the Nobel Prize for anything – literature, peace, science? The obedient child becomes just the common crowd. All that is added to existence is added by the disobedient.

Obsession

Obsession simply means you are paying too much attention and energy to something which is not that important. You have become focused on something out of all proportion.

Obsession is a kind of hypnosis that you have created within yourself. Then everything disappears in your life apart from one thing, your focal point. Your life becomes one-dimensional: that is obsession.

There are people who think only of sex, only of sex 24 hours a day. It is always lurking deep down in their minds. They may be doing something else, but they are thinking of sex. Then it is an obsession. Sex itself is not an obsession, remember. I am not against sex. I am not against anything. But an obsession with sex means that sex has taken the place of everything. There are also people who are obsessed with food; they are continuously thinking of food ... Obsession means something becoming your whole life.

Nothing should become your whole life. Everything has its own place. Life should be an orchestra. Life should be multi-dimensional.

Occultism

Occult means 'that which is hidden' – and we are always interested in the hidden. But nothing is hidden! God is not hidden; God is very much manifest. He is all over the place: singing in the birds, flowering in the flowers. He is green in the trees, red in the roses. He is breathing in you. He is talking through me and listening through you right this very moment. As far as God is concerned, nothing is hidden. Just open your eyes and he is standing before you. But you don't want to see the obvious.

Why go into occultism to explore inner space? Why not go directly into inner space? Be silent and you will hear the still, small voice within yourself.

Occultism is so much nonsense, and there is no end to it because it is all invention. It is religious fiction. Just as there is science fiction, so occultism is religious fiction. If you love fiction, it is perfectly OK. But don't think that by reading science fiction you are studying science. And don't believe in science fiction, and don't act out of that belief, otherwise you will end up in a madhouse.

People love fiction; there is nothing wrong in it, but you should know that it is fiction. Enjoy, but don't take it seriously.

Optimism

Mullah Nasruddin constantly irritated his friends with his eternal optimism. No matter how bad the situation, he would always say, 'It could have been worse.' To cure him of this annoying habit his friends decided to invent a situation so completely black, so dreadful that even Nasruddin could find no hope in it.

Approaching him at the club bar one day, one of them said, 'Mullah, did you hear what happened to George? He went home last night, found his wife in bed with another man, shot them both, then turned the gun on himself.'

'Terrible,' said the Mullah, 'but it could have been worse.'

'How the hell,' asked his dumbfounded friend, 'could it possibly have been worse?'

'Well,' said Nasruddin, 'if it had happened the day before, I would be dead now.'

The first thing to understand about optimism and pessimism is that they are not different. They look different, but don't be deceived by appearances. They are just two polarities of the same phenomenon. A pessimist can become an optimist; an optimist can become a pessimist. A pessimist is just an optimist standing on his head, and vice versa. They are not two different people, they are not two different dimensions. Remember, it is not worth changing rooms. Get out of both, under the sky where neither pessimism nor optimism exist. You can be at ease only when both are gone, because both are wrong.

Take any situation. The pessimist looks at the darker side of things and denies the lighter side; he accepts only half of the truth. The optimist denies the darker side of things and accepts only the lighter side; he is also half true. Neither of them accepts the whole truth, because the whole truth is both summer and winter, God and Devil, darkness and light, good and evil, life and death. The whole truth is both. Both optimist and pessimist are doing the same thing – they are denying the half and accepting the other half. The other half is as much half as the first; there is no difference. If the pessimist is wrong, the optimist is also wrong. Neither is ready to accept the truth as it is. They choose.

Don't choose. Move out of both and go under the open sky of choicelessness. Let truth be as it is. Don't try to paint it in your own mood. Don't look through hope, don't look through frustration. Don't be positive and don't be negative – that is the highest consciousness possible.

Orgasm

Sexual orgasm is the lowest but most fundamental experience of meditation. It is through sexual orgasm that man became aware of the possibility of stopping time completely, of getting out of time. If you can get out of time for one moment, that means you can get out of time forever too. Once people became aware of this possibility, ways and means had to be found. That's how Tantra, Yoga, Zen, Tao, Sufism were found.

So once in a while you may have become aware that time stops, but time stops only when you are blissful. Time stops only when you are absolutely without mind – conscious, yet without mind because you are not 'minding', you are not thinking …

It can happen in music, it can happen while watching a sunset, it can happen while you are painting. But experiencing it then is far more rare than experiencing it through sex. Sex is available to each and everybody; it is a biological gift of nature.

Original Face

Zen people say, 'Find out your face, the face you had before you were born; find out that face that you will again have when you are dead. Between birth and death, whatever you think is your face is accidental. You have seen it in a mirror. You have not felt it from within, you have looked at it from without.'

Do you know your original face? You know only the face the mirror shows to you. And all our relationships are just mirrors. You see your own original face in deep silence.

Original Sin

Sex has been called the original sin, but it is neither original nor sin. Even before Adam and Eve ate the fruit from the Tree of Knowledge they were having sex and all the other animals in the Garden of Eden were having sex. The only thing that happened after the eating of the fruit of knowledge was awareness. Adam and Eve became aware of it and by becoming aware of it they became ashamed.

Now Christians say Adam and Eve committed the original sin and the whole of humanity is suffering as a result.

That is so patently foolish! Scientists say that humanity has existed for millions of years. Millions of years ago, a couple, Adam and Eve, committed a sin and we are suffering as a result? Can you think of anything more ridiculous than that you are now imprisoned because millions of years ago somebody committed a crime? You did not commit it; how can you suffer for it? What original sin are they talking about? It is neither original nor sin.

Pagan

The first thing to understand is, who is a pagan? A pagan is not what Christians call a pagan. A pagan is a natural man – sincere, not a hypocrite, living life naturally, not dominated by the mind. He is part of existence. He is always moving with existence, wherever it leads, rather than trying to go in some other direction.

There is no goal in the life of a pagan. No question about meaning arises in the life of a pagan. Life in itself is so beautiful that to question its meaning is simply pointless.

Pain

Pain is part of growth. And remember, whenever something hurts, something inside you is repressed. So rather than trying to avoid the pain, move into it. Let it hurt like hell. Let it hurt totally so the wound is opened completely. Once it is opened completely, it starts healing. If you avoid the spaces when you feel pain, they will remain inside you and you will come across them again and again.

Palmistry

All palmistry, all astrology, all forms of divination are just exploitation of our anguish. Because we are in anguish we want somehow somebody to tell us what we are, what we are going to be, what our future is.

It is out of anguish that all these sciences have sprung up. And they have exploited people for thousands of years, for the simple reason that everyone is bound sometime or other to be concerned with what this life is all about: 'What am I doing here? Is it really meaningful or meaningless? Is it leading me somewhere or am I moving in a circle? And if it is leading somewhere, am I going in the right direction or in the wrong direction?'

Paradise

Everybody is searching for paradise. You can give it different names – nirvana, enlightenment, *samadhi,* the Kingdom of God, ultimate truth – and you can go on giving it different names, but you will still be missing it – missing not because you have been thrown out of the Garden of Eden, but missing because you are in the garden and you have fallen into a deep dreamlike state. The dream consists of your desire to be somewhere else, to reach the peaks.

My insistence is that you are already there, in paradise. Just sit silently and look around you, sit silently and look within. You have never been anywhere else! The way you are is the only way you can be. Accept it – and not only accept it but rejoice in it, love it, and suddenly you will find you are awake in the Garden of Eden. It is not a question of going anywhere, just of being here now.

Paradox

Mystics use the word 'paradox', not contradiction. In the very word 'contradiction' there is a condemnation:

something is wrong, something has to be put right. But a paradox is a totally different phenomenon. Nothing has to be put right. A paradox is a mystery, elusive, inexplicable.

Existence is a mystery. Mathematics is incapable of understanding it; the mind is incapable of understanding it, utterly incapable, because the mind knows only one way. The Aristotelian way is the mind's way. And anybody who knows life knows that Aristotle has been a calamity, the greatest calamity that has ever existed in the world. And he is the father of modern philosophy, the father of modern science! But now there is a revolt against his ideas. Mystics have always been revolting, now the physicists are revolting.

Past

The mind lives in the past because it lives in knowledge. Knowledge means that which you have known, understood, learned. And existence is now and the mind is then, existence is here and the mind is there. The mind looks backwards; it is like a rearview mirror. If you are backing your car the rearview mirror is OK, but if you are going forwards then it is dangerous to go on looking in the rearview mirror. And if you become fixated on the rearview mirror you are bound to have an accident. You are in great danger, you are being suicidal. Life always moves forwards; there is no possibility of going backwards.

Path

One path to truth – the path of self-cultivation – is a time-bound path, it has nothing to do with eternity. And truth is eternity.

The second path, the path of enlightenment, Zen masters have always called the 'pathless path' because it does not appear to be a path at all. It cannot appear as a path, but just for the purposes of communication we will arbitrarily call it 'the second path'. The second path is not part of time, it is part of eternity. So it happens instantaneously; it happens in the present. You cannot desire it, you cannot be ambitious for it. It is said that the path of enlightenment is like a bird flying in the sky: it leaves no footprints behind it. Every bird will have to make its own footprints, but they disappear immediately as the bird flies.

Perfection

I am not a perfectionist because to me perfectionism is the root cause of all neurosis. Unless we get rid of the idea of perfection we are never going to be sane. The very idea of perfection has driven the whole of humanity to a state of madness. To think in terms of perfection means you are thinking in terms of ideology, goals, values, shoulds, should nots. You have a certain pattern to fulfil and if you stray from that pattern you will feel immensely guilty, a sinner. And the pattern is bound to be such that you cannot achieve it. If you can achieve it, then it will not be of much value to the ego.

So the intrinsic quality of the perfectionist ideal is that it should be unattainable – only then is it worth attaining. You see the contradiction? And that contradiction creates a sort of schizophrenia: you are trying to do the impossible, which you know perfectly well is not going to happen – it cannot happen in the very nature of things ...

So only two alternatives are left. One is that you start feeling guilty. If you are innocent, simple, intelligent, you will start feeling guilty – and guilt is a state of sickness ... The second alternative is that if you are cunning then you will become a hypocrite, you will start pretending that you have achieved your ideal. You will deceive others and you will even try to deceive yourself. You will start living an illusion, a hallucination.

Personality

Personality as such is false. The word 'personality' has to be understood. It comes from *persona*, which means a mask. In ancient Greek drama the actors used to wear masks and those masks were called *persona* – *persona* because the sound came from behind the mask. *Sona* means sound.

Like the mask, the *persona*, all personality is false. A good personality, a bad personality, the personality of a sinner, the personality of a saint, all are false. You can wear a beautiful mask or an ugly mask, it doesn't make any difference, it's still a mask.

Enlightenment is the dropping of the personality.

Philosophy

Aristotle says that philosophy begins in wonder, but it's not so in the East. In the East, nobody has ever said that philosophy begins in wonder. In the East we say that philosophy begins in the awareness of suffering, not in wonder; in the anguish of man, not in wonder. Philosophy begins in the angst of man, in the meaninglessness of man's life and in the awareness of it.

So Western philosophy has remained a kind of entertainment. Eastern philosophy is not entertainment – it is work, it is *sadhana*. In fact there is no word in any language to translate this Indian word *sadhana* because nothing like it has ever existed anywhere else. *Sadhana* means that philosophy is not just thinking, but *being*. You have to become your philosophy, you have to live it! It has to become your blood and bones and marrow. *Sadhana* has to become your way of life. Whatever you think is right has to be lived – that is the only proof that you think it is right. If you think that something is right and you live otherwise, then you are fooling others and you are fooling yourself.

Poverty

In the past we have praised poverty and made it equal to spirituality, which is absolute nonsense.

You can live in absolute poverty, but poverty cannot help you to enlightenment. In poverty or in wealth, in a hut or in a palace, the basic thing is your meditation, your awareness. Wherever it happens, you will become enlightened. You don't have to renounce riches, you don't have to renounce anything.

Remember that all the religions have been serving the poor for thousands of years, and poverty goes on growing. Real service is telling the poor to revolt against vested interests.

Prayer

I know only of one prayer and that is absolute silence. The moment you say something you have destroyed it, so the prayers that are said in the churches and the temples and the mosques and the synagogues are not true prayers.

Why say anything? What is there to say to the whole? The whole knows it already. Before we know it, the whole knows it. It is just stupid to go on saying things to God. It is meaningless.

As far as the whole is concerned, language is meaningless, language has to be put aside. And to put aside language means to put everything aside – your mind, your knowledge, your scriptures, your religion, your church – because they all belong to the world of language. Simply sit silently.

Priests

When a child grows up he starts doubting that his father knows everything – and he is right. He starts finding out that his father is not infallible, that he commits mistakes, that there are many people who are far stronger than him. Up to now he has trusted in his father and been at ease. Now a great unease arises in him. He has become dependent on a father figure for protection. He needs a father who is all-powerful, ever-present, omnipotent. This is the root cause of the projection of God.

The priest exploits this situation. He says God is far away and to know God needs tremendous discipline, hard work and continuous prayer, so that only those very few people who can go through all those austerities can come close to God. Only the priests have a direct communication line. They will mediate for you.

The priest always has a strong hold, because the priest is the most ancient institution in the world. They say the most ancient profession in the world is that of the prostitute. I don't agree. The most ancient profession is that of the priest, because without the priest who will create the prostitute?

Psychology

Psychology is a very ordinary phenomenon. It does not bring transformation to your life because it cannot bring transcendence. At the most it helps you to be a little more adjusted to yourself and to the world around you, to society and to the people with whom you have to live.

Psychology is basically orthodox; it is not revolutionary, it cannot be. It serves the status quo, it serves the establishment. It keeps you within the boundaries; it does not help you to go beyond the boundaries. It is not in your service. It is controlled by those who are in power – by the state, by the church, by society. In a very disguised way it keeps you tethered to the collective mind.

Quest

Life is a quest, not a question; a mystery, not a problem. And the difference is vast. A problem has to be solved, can be solved, must be solved, but a mystery is insoluble; it has to be lived, experienced. A question has to be answered so that it disappears; encountering a mystery, you have to dissolve in it. The mystery remains, you disappear. It is a totally different phenomenon. In philosophy the problem disappears, but *you* remain; in religiousness the mystery remains, you disappear, you evaporate.

The ego is very interested in questions and very afraid of the mystery. Questions arise out of the ego. It plays with questions, tries to find out answers, and each answer in its own turn brings more questions. It is an unending process; that's why philosophy has not come to any conclusions …

Questions are nourishment for the mind.

Question

Once a rabbi was asked by a Christian priest, 'Rabbi, will you please give me a straight answer to a straight question? Why is it that the Jews always answer a question by asking one?'

The rabbi reflected for a moment, then replied, 'Do they?'

Rebellion

Intelligence is rebellion. The intelligent person is rebellious. The intelligent person decides on his own whether to say no or yes. The intelligent person cannot be traditional, he cannot go on worshipping the past; there is nothing to worship in the past. The intelligent person does not cling to the dead past, does not carry corpses. However beautiful they were, however precious, he does not carry the corpses. He is finished with the past; it is gone, and it is gone forever.

The intelligent person wants to create a future, wants to live in the present. Living in the present is his way of creating the future.

(and/or)

Reform means a modification. The old remains, you give it a new form, a new shape – a kind of renovation of an old building. Its original structure remains; you whitewash it, you clean it, you make a few windows, a few new doors. Revolution goes deeper than reform. The old remains, but more changes are introduced, even in its basic structure. You are not only changing the colour of the building and opening a few windows and doors, you are adding new floors, taking it higher into the sky. But the old is not destroyed, it remains hidden behind the new; in fact, it remains the very foundation of the new.

Revolution is a continuity with the old. Rebellion is a discontinuity. It is not reform, it is not revolution, it is simply disconnecting yourself from all that is old. The old religions, the old political ideologies, the old man – you disconnect yourself from all that is old. You start life afresh, from scratch.

The birth of a rebel is the death of the old. The revolutionary tries to change the old; the rebel simply comes out of the old, just as the snake slips out of the old skin, and never looks back. To me, rebelliousness is the essential quality of a religious man. It is spirituality in its absolute purity.

Rebirth

Jesus says to Nicodemus, 'Unless you are born again you will not enter into the Kingdom of God.' He also says, 'Unless you are like a child you will not enter into the Kingdom of God.' What does he mean? He simply means that a rebirth is needed.

The moment that you are awake, everything becomes a mystery. Suddenly all knowledge evaporates like dewdrops in the early morning sun. For the first time your eyes are full of wonder like those of a child. It is a second birth. In India we call the person who comes to know the mystery of existence *dwij* – twice born.

Reflection

Reflection is nothing but a beautiful word for thinking. The blind man can go on thinking about light, and he can arrive at certain conclusions too, but those conclusions cannot be right. However right they appear to be, they are bound to be false.

The moon in the sky is one thing and the moon reflected in the lake is totally another. One exists, the other is only a reflection. If you jump into the lake you will not be able to catch hold of the moon; on the contrary, you may even disturb its reflection because the lake will be disturbed.

The more you think, the more you are creating waves and ripples in the mind. The real thing for the blind man to do is not to think about light but to heal his eyes, for the deaf man it is not to reflect on music but to go through some alchemical process that can make him hear.

Relativity

A man who was frightened of dentists delayed seeing one until he only had six teeth left in his mouth. The dentist examined him and said, 'These teeth are finished. Let me do some root canal work, implants and all those other things I do, and you'll have a complete new set of choppers. You'll look beautiful and you won't have any more problems chewing.'

The man was dubious. 'I'm a physical coward. I can't stand pain.'

'Who said anything about pain? I'm a painless dentist!'

'*You* say so, but how do I know if it's true?'

'Not to worry,' the dentist said. 'I did a job exactly like this for another man. I'll give you his name and you can phone him right now. Ask if I caused him any pain.'

So the man telephoned George Kaplan in Brooklyn. 'Mr Kaplan,' he said, 'my name is Al Goldstein. You don't know me, but I'm with your dentist and he says he did a big job on your teeth. Is that correct?'

'It is correct,' Kaplan agreed.

'OK,' said Goldstein. 'Now I want you to tell me the honest truth. Did it hurt? Tell me, yes or no?'

'A "yes" or "no" I can't give you,' said Kaplan. 'But I can give you a "for instance". Every Sunday I go rowing in Prospect Park.'

'So?' said Goldstein.

'So,' said Kaplan, 'our dentist finished with me in December. Now it's June and it's Sunday, and as usual I'm in my boat on the Prospect Park lake. Suddenly, one of the oars slips away. When I reach over to grab it, my balls get caught in the oarlock. Would you believe it, Mr Goldstein, it was the first time in six months that my teeth didn't hurt!'

That's what the theory of relativity is.

Relaxation

Many people would like to relax, but they cannot. Relaxation is like a flowering: you cannot force it. You have to understand the whole phenomenon – why you are so active, why you are so occupied with activity, why you are obsessed with it.

Relaxation means that this moment is more than enough, more than can be asked or expected. It's more than you can desire – and so your energy doesn't move anywhere. It becomes a placid pool. You dissolve in it. That moment is relaxation.

Relaxation is neither of the body nor of the mind, relaxation is total. That's why Buddhas go on saying, 'Lose all desire,' because they know that if there is any desire, you cannot relax. They go on saying, 'Bury the dead,' because if you are too concerned with the past, you cannot relax. They go on saying, 'Enjoy this very moment.'

Jesus says, 'Consider the lilies of the field – they toil not and neither do they spin, yet even King Solomon in all his splendour was not arrayed like one of these.' What is he saying? He is saying, 'Relax! You need not toil – in fact, everything is provided.'

Jesus says, 'If he looks after the birds of the air, the animals, wild animals, trees and plants, then why are you worried? Will he not look after you?' That is relaxation. Why are you so worried about the future? Consider the lilies and become like lilies – and then relax.

Relaxation is not a posture; relaxation is a total transformation of your energy.

Religion

The word 'religion' is very beautiful. It comes from a root, *religere*, which means 'to rejoin', 'to reunite'. With whom? With yourself, with the source of your being. And why reunite? Because you are already united with the source, so it is a reunion. You have come from the source. Deep down you are still in the source. Just on the periphery, it is as if the branches of a tree have forgotten about the roots – not that they are broken from the roots, because then they cannot live. They have simply forgotten the roots are there. In their ego, in their height in the sky, in their romance with the moon, they have completely forgotten that they have roots underground, which nourish them, which sustain them, without which they cannot exist for a single moment. And all the greenery, and all the flowers, and all the fruit will simply disappear like dreams once they are cut from the root.

That's how it happens to you. You move in the branches, farther and farther away from the roots. You come to many flowers. You are enchanted. All around you the world is beautiful. You completely forget about the roots, but it is not that you are uprooted. Forgetfulness is just forgetfulness.

And that is the meaning of religion: to reunite, to remember again. This word 'remember' is also beautiful. It means to become a member again, re-member – to become part of the source again, to go to the source and become a member of it again. Religion is remembering, becoming once more a part of the organic unity that you are.

Religion is reuniting with your own source. It is not concerned with others, it is concerned with you, absolutely with you. Religion is personal. It is not a social phenomenon. The ego is always concerned with others. When you become totally concerned with yourself, the ego simply drops away. There is no reason for it to exist.

Religion is when you are so alone that there is nobody left to be met. In that total, virgin aloneness, supreme ecstasy is born.

Remembering

Think about the word 'remembering'. It really means becoming part again of the whole, becoming a member again of the family that is existence.

Remembering means that we suddenly learn the language that we had forgotten. It is like a forgotten name: you see somebody on the road, you recognize him, you feel that you know who he is, but you cannot remember his name. You have forgotten, although you can remember that you know him, that you've met him before. You say, 'His name is just on the tip of my tongue.' But if it is on the tip of your tongue, then why is it not coming? And then you try to remember it and the harder you try, the more difficult it becomes, because whenever you try to do something very hard you become tense, you become closed, your consciousness becomes narrower and narrower. And it becomes more and more difficult to remember. Then you drop the whole project, thinking that it is not possible. You forget all about it. You start listening to music or you go into the garden and you sit under a tree or you start doing something else, sipping tea or talking to somebody … and then suddenly from nowhere the name surfaces.

This is the whole secret of enlightenment: it happens in relaxation, it happens in a deep state of rest.

Renunciation

I wonder that people like Gautama Buddha, Mahavira and others, have insisted that the quality of the outer world is just like rainbows, dreams, and have still renounced it! If they understand that the world is just a dream, then there is no point in renouncing it. Do you renounce your dreams every morning? You know they were dreams and that's that!

You need not escape from the rainbows. They are beautiful and they exist only for the moment. Why long for them to be permanent? What is wrong in their being momentary?

Just rejoice! Enjoy the rainbows! When it rains, just dance in the rainbows.

Repentance

The word 'repent' has to be understood; it has been misunderstood down the ages. Jesus said again and again, 'Repent! Repent because the end of the world is nigh.' When Jesus' statements were translated into English from the Greek, many of the words suffered as a consequence. The word 'repent' suffered the most. It is a translation of a Greek word, *metanoia*. *Metanoia* means 'turning in', 'meditation'. 'To repent' also means 'to return' – return to the source. It has nothing to do with the idea of repentance that you have been taught in your churches. To repent means to turn in, to return, to go back to the source of your being, to the very core of your being.

Repression

Repression is living a life you were not meant to live. Repression is doing things you never wanted to do. Repression is being a person you are not; it is a way of destroying yourself. Repression is suicide – very slow of course, but very certain, a slow poisoning.

Expression is life; repression is suicide.

Don't live a repressed life, otherwise you're not living at all. Live a life of expression, creativity, joy. Live the natural way. Listen to your instincts, listen to your body, listen to your heart, listen to your intelligence. Depend on yourself, go wherever your spontaneity takes you, and you will never be at a loss. And going spontaneously with your natural life, one day you are bound to arrive at the doors of the divine.

Response

What is response? Response is unprogrammed; it is experiencing in the moment. You look at a flower – you *really* look at the flower, with no ideas covering your eyes. You look at *this* flower, the *thisness* of it, with all knowledge put aside. Your heart responds. Your mind reacts. You may not say anything; in fact, there is no need to say 'This flower is beautiful.' Response is of the heart. Response is a feeling, not a thought. You are thrilled. Seeing a flower something starts dancing in you, something is stirred at the deepest core of your being. Something starts opening inside you. The outer flower challenges the inner flower, and the inner flower responds.

And if you are not engaged in trivialities, you will have enough energy to have this inner dance of the heart. When energy is dissipated in thoughts, your feelings are starved. Thoughts are parasites: they live on the energy which is really meant for the feelings; they exploit it. Thoughts are like leakages in your being, they take your energy away. Then you are like a pot with holes – you cannot contain anything.

When thoughts are not taking your energy away, its level starts rising higher and higher. You can contain your energy. You have a kind of fullness. And in that fullness the heart responds.

Responsibility

Responsibility means the ability to respond. It does not mean a duty. Go to the root meaning of the word: it means 'to be responsive'.

Love is a response. When the other calls, you are ready. When the other invites, you enter. When the other does not invite, you don't trespass. When the other sings, you sing in response. When the other offers a hand to you, you take it with deep response.

Responsibility means openness, readiness to respond.

Reverence

I have no philosophy of non-violence, but I have a way of life which you can call reverence for life. And this is a totally different perspective. Non-violence simply says don't kill others. Do you think that is enough? It is only a negative statement: don't kill others, don't harm others. Is that enough? Reverence for life says share, give your joy, your love, your peace, your bliss. Whatever you can share, share.

If you are reverent towards life then it becomes a form of worship. Then watching a tree becomes worship. Then feeding a guest becomes worship.

If we can learn to understand our inner being, we will have great compassion and love for every being. We will have a tremendous reverence for life.

Revolution

Revolution is a spiritual phenomenon. There can be no political revolution, no social revolution, no economic revolution. Revolution is only possible in the individual soul. Social revolution is a pseudo phenomenon, because society has no soul of its own. The only revolution is that of the spirit; it is individual. And if millions of individuals change, then society will change as a consequence, not vice versa. You cannot change society first and hope that individuals will change later on. That's why revolutions have been failing, because we have looked at revolution from the wrong perspective. We have thought that if you change society, then one day the individuals, the constituent elements of society, will change. This is stupid. Who is going to start such a revolution?

Riches

I have been poor and I have been rich. And believe me, it is far better to be rich than poor. I am a man of very simple tastes. I am utterly satisfied with the best, I don't ask for more.

Roots

To grow up, just watch a tree. As a tree grows up, its roots grow down. There is a balance: the higher the tree goes, the deeper the roots will go. You cannot have a tree 150 feet high with small roots; they could not support such a huge tree.

In life, growing up means growing deep within yourself – that's where your roots are.

Sacred

Nothing in the world is more sacred than tears of love and joy. Such tears, so pure, are not of this world. Though part of the body, they express something which is not of the body.

Sacrifice

A single moment of passionate love, of passionate living, of passionate stillness, is more valuable than the whole of eternity. It is a question of how to live this moment, it is not a question of survival. The idea of survival makes tomorrow more important than today, makes it easier for you to sacrifice today for tomorrow. And tomorrow never comes – whenever it comes, it is today. And if your mind is programmed to sacrifice today for tomorrow, you go on sacrificing your whole life.

Parents sacrifice their lives for their children. The children again in their turn will sacrifice their lives for their children, and so on and so forth. And nobody will ever live.

I am against the very idea of sacrifice. Never sacrifice! Live this moment; live it totally, intensely, passionately. And then a miracle happens: if parents have lived their life beautifully, if they are fulfilled, their very fulfilment creates the space for their children to live in the right way. And by the right way I don't mean the moral way, I mean the total way. To live partially is to live wrongly, to live totally is to live rightly.

Saints

I am against so-called saints – I am trying to create real saints. The saints that I criticize are not saints of love. They are all anti-love, anti-life; they are not life-affirmative. Real saintliness cannot be against love and against life. It can't be against this celebration that goes on and on. If somebody is full of life's joy and love for life, then that is real saintliness.

Real saintliness is a participation in existence as it is. The real sage or saint will not choose, he will accept whatever is given. The body is given, so he will accept it. The world is given, so he will accept it, and he will accept it with immense gratitude, because it is God's gift.

Real saints will not be recognized as saints; no church will sanctify them. And the saints that are sanctified by the church are really bogus, mumbo-jumbo, false, artificial, synthetic, plastic saints. They don't laugh. But Jesus laughed, he drank, he ate well, he loved. He was a true man of the earth, very earthly, rooted in the earth.

Salvation

If Jesus had been a meditator, things would have been totally different. He would not have declared that he was the only begotten son of God. He would not have declared that he was the messiah the Jews had been awaiting for centuries. He would not have declared that he had come to redeem humanity, that he was a saviour. These are impossible statements for a man of meditation.

A man of meditation knows there is no God. He knows there is godliness – a quality but not a person; not like a flower but like a fragrance. And godliness is all over, you just have to be alert and awake at the centre of your being. There is no question of the only begotten son.

And the meditator knows that nobody can save you except yourself because nobody can enter your centre. That is your privilege and your privacy. You can be killed, but nobody can touch your innermost being, for good or ill.

A meditator cannot say 'I can save you' or 'I can save the whole of humanity' or 'I am your saviour.' A meditator cannot say 'I am a messiah, a messenger' because there is no God sending messiahs and messengers.

A meditator can do only one thing: he can make himself available to you with all his joy, with all his grace, with all his beauty. He can remind you in a certain way that the same reality lies asleep within you. He can become a pointer. He can be a finger pointing to the moon, but he cannot take you to the moon.

Even to try and convince you is not possible for the meditator. He can only communicate. He can say, 'I have found something. Perhaps you can find it too. Just look within.' He can tell you how he has looked within himself and how he has found the very source of life.

But he is not a prophet. He does not claim any speciality, he does not claim that he is higher than you. He says he is as ordinary as you, with just a little difference – that he has opened his eyes and you are still snoring.

Search

Every child is born with an innate search for truth. It is not something learned or adopted later on in life. It is natural.

Truth simply means, 'I am, but I do not know who I am. I must know the reality of my being.'

The search for truth is really the search for the reality of your being.

Secrets

All that is beautiful is inner, and inner means privacy. Have you watched women making love? They always close their eyes. They know something. A man makes love with his eyes open; he remains a watcher. He is not completely in the act, he is not totally in it. He remains a voyeur. But a woman knows better because she is more delicately tuned to the inner world. She always closes her eyes. Then love has a totally different fragrance …

Secrecy has its own reason for being there. Remember that, and remember that you will behave very foolishly in life if you become completely public. It will be as if you had turned your pockets inside-out. That will be your shape – like pockets turned inside-out. There is nothing wrong with being open, facing outward, but remember that is only part of life. It should not become the whole.

Self

The ego is a substitute self. Because we are not aware of the true self, we create the ego, even though it is make-believe.

And because we cannot live without a centre we have to invent a false centre. There are two possibilities: either know the true centre or create a false centre. Society encourages the creation of the false centre because the false person can easily be dominated – and he will seek to be dominated. He is constantly in search of somebody to dominate him. Only when he is dominated does he have a certain feeling of worth. His worth, his life, all are borrowed. He has no meaning in his life on his own; somebody else has to give meaning to him. He becomes part of a church, then he feels good. He is a Christian, and Christianity gives him a sense of meaning, or he becomes a communist and the crowd of communists helps him to feel that he is doing something important. He cannot stand alone.

That is the whole strategy of society: it does not allow you to stand on your own. It cripples you, from the very beginning it makes you dependent on crutches. And the best way to do it is not to allow you to become aware of your true self.

So instead of the true self society gives you a toy called the ego. It supports the ego tremendously; society praises the ego, nourishes it. If you follow the dictates of society in every possible way you will be respected, and respectability is nothing but food for the ego. If you don't follow the dictates of society, you will not be respected. That is punishing your ego, keeping it starved, and it is very difficult to live like that, so you are ready to fulfil all kinds of demands, rational or irrational.

My effort is to help you to drop this false entity called the ego. Dropping it is half of the work and the other half is easier: becoming aware of your true self. Once the false is seen as false, it is not very difficult to see the true as true.

Sensitivity

Becoming is the disease of the soul.

Being is you.

And to discover your being is the beginning of life. Then each moment is a new discovery, each moment brings a new joy, a new mystery opens its doors, a new love starts growing in you, a new compassion that you have never felt before, a new sensitivity about beauty, about goodness.

You become so sensitive that even the smallest blade of grass takes on an immense importance for you. Your sensitivity makes it clear to you that this small blade of grass is as important to existence as the biggest star; without this blade of grass, existence would be less than it is. And this small blade of grass is unique, it is irreplaceable, it has its own individuality.

And this sensitivity will create new friendships for you – friendships with trees, with birds, with animals, with mountains, with rivers, with oceans, with stars. Life becomes richer as friendliness grows, as love grows.

In the life of St Francis, there is a beautiful incident. St Francis has always travelled on a donkey from place to place sharing his experiences. Now he is dying. All his disciples are gathered to listen to his last words. The last words of a man are always the most significant that he ever utters because they contain the whole experience of his life. But the disciples cannot believe what they are hearing …

St Francis does not address the disciples; he addresses the donkey. He says, 'Brother, I am immensely indebted to you. You have been carrying me from one place to another place with never a complaint, never a grumble. Before I leave this world, all that I want is forgiveness from you. I have not been humane to you.'

These were the last words of St Francis. What tremendous sensitivity to call the donkey 'brother' and ask to be forgiven.

As you become more sensitive, life becomes bigger. It is not a small pond, it becomes oceanic. It is not confined to you and your wife and your children – it is not confined at all. The whole of existence becomes your family and unless the whole of existence is your family you have not known what life is.

No man is an island, we are all connected. We are a vast continent, joined in millions of ways.

And if our hearts are not full of love for the whole, in the same proportion our life is cut short.

Meditation will bring you sensitivity and a great sense of belonging to the world. It is our world. We are not foreigners here. We belong to existence. We are part of it, we are *heart* of it.

Sensuality

Get more into your body. Make your senses more alive. See more lovingly, taste more lovingly, touch more lovingly, smell more lovingly. Let your senses function more and more. Then suddenly you will see that the excess energy that was in your head has spread throughout your body.

The head is very dictatorial. It goes on taking energy from everywhere. It is a monopolist. It has killed the senses. The head takes almost 80 per cent of your energy and only 20 per cent is left for the rest of your body. Of course the whole body suffers as a result, because you can only be happy when you are functioning as a whole, as an organic unity, and every part of your body and being is getting its just proportion of energy, no more, no less. Then you function in rhythm. You are in harmony.

Harmony, happiness, health – they are all part of one phenomenon and that is wholeness. If you are whole, you are happy, healthy, harmonious.

Seriousness

Those who take life seriously become pathological, because life is not a serious phenomenon. It is all playfulness, from top to bottom. It is a song to be sung, a dance to be danced, a love to be loved – but with utter playfulness.

The moment you become serious you become blocked, the flow stops, you are cut off from the universal energy. You cannot dance when you are serious because seriousness is basically sadness. Seriousness is also calculation, business. Whenever you do something you are always asking, 'Why do it? What am I going to get out of it? What will the profit be?' These are businesslike attitudes. They are good in the marketplace but they are absolutely wrong when you start moving inwards. The more you move inwards, the more life appears to be fun, tremendous fun. A sense of humour is needed and a sense of playfulness.

In the past just the opposite has been the case: the saints have been very sad and very serious, as if life were a burden, a heavy burden, as if they were carrying mountains on their heads. They were not free like children, playing for no reason at all, playing just for playing's sake ...

Sex

Sex is so significant because it is the source of all life. It is so significant that if you repress it you will repress many other things as well. For example, the person who is sexually repressed will become uncreative, because creativity itself is a kind of sexual activity.

In my observation, if a person is totally creative he will transcend sex without repressing it, because his own energy will become creative. The very need for sex will disappear. A far higher bliss will be happening to him and the lower is bound to disappear when you have the higher. A real poet, while producing, creating, composing, forgets all about sex. A real sculptor absorbed in his work forgets all about sex. Even if a naked woman passes by he will not look at her, his concentration is so total. A real dancer disappears in his dance. His ego, his sex drive, everything is dissolved into his dance.

But if sex is repressed, then just the contrary will be the result: your creativity will be repressed, and the implications of repressed creativity are very great, multi-dimensional ... If your creativity is repressed, all your scientific endeavour will disappear too. But if your sex life is flowing joyously, you will have tremendous interest in everything you are doing ...

According to me, sex is the seed. If it is allowed natural growth, respected, valued, then a transformation happens, a metamorphosis. Sex starts growing foliage of art, music, poetry, dance, and thousand other creative dimensions. Sex is only a seed, or the roots, but if supported, nourished, watered, taken care of, then many branches grow, with thick foliage, many green leaves moving in all directions, dancing in the wind, in the rain, in the sun ... This is the world of art, the world of aesthetics. And if you allow the world of aesthetics to reach its highest peak, then flowers will bloom.

Sexuality

Sexuality is a very great thing. By sexuality I mean whenever your body is alive, sensuous, throbbing, pulsating – then you are in a sexual state. It may not have anything to do with a genital experience. The genital is only one very, very tiny expression of the sexual. For example, when you are dancing you are sexual, the energy is sexual energy, but it is not genital. You may not be thinking about sex, you may have completely forgotten about sex, but in fact when you are involved in any deep participation with your total body, it is sexual, it is sexuality.

So when I use the word 'sexual' I mean this experience of totality. By and by sexuality has become confined to the genitals; it has become local, it is no longer total. This is ugly because the most it can give you is relief; it can never give you orgasm. Ejaculation is not orgasm, not all ejaculations are orgasmic and not every orgasm is a peak experience. Ejaculation is genital, orgasm is sexual and a peak experience is spiritual.

When sexuality is confined to the genitals you can only have relief; you simply lose energy, you don't gain anything. It is just like the relief that comes out of a good sneeze, no more than that. It is not an orgasm because your total body does not pulsate. You are not in a dance, you are not participating with your whole being, it is not holy. It is very partial and the partial can never be orgasmic because orgasm is possible only when the total organism is involved. When you pulsate from your toe to your head, when every fibre of your being pulsates, when all the cells of your body dance, when there is a great orchestra inside you, that is orgasm. But not every orgasm is a peak experience. When you are pulsating totally inside, it is an orgasm. When your totality participates with the totality of existence, it is a peak experience. And people are focused on ejaculation, they have forgotten orgasm and they have completely forgotten the peak experience. They don't know what it is. And because they cannot attain the higher, they are confined to the lower.

When you can attain the higher, when you can attain the better, naturally the lower starts disappearing of its own accord. So, sex is transformed, but not sexuality. As sex disappears you will become more sexual.

Where will sex go? It will become your sexuality. You will become more sensuous. You will live with more intensity, with more flame; you will live like a great wave. These tiny waves will disappear. You will become a storm, you will become a great wind that can shake the trees and the mountains. You will be a tide, a flood. Your candle will burn at both ends together, simultaneously.

And in that moment you will have a taste of eternity.

Shyness

Shyness is always the by-product of a very subtle ego. With the familiar, the ego knows what to do and how to remain in power, so you are skilful. With the unfamiliar, with the unknown, the ego is at a loss because it has no skills for the unknown. So it shrinks, withdraws, and that shrinking feeling is called shyness. The more egoistic you are, the shyer you are, because you cannot open yourself to new situations. New situations may prove you to be a fool. New situations may embarrass you, they may take away the very ground from underneath you.

So shyness is never really a problem in itself, it is just a symptom. But down the ages it has been thought to be a good quality – because it protects the ego! We think a shy person is a good person, a non-aggressive person, but this is not so. A shy person's aggression is very subtle. Shy people are aloof, they always keep their distance. That distance is just a strategy; if things become too much they can always escape. They never get involved, they remain on the periphery and pretend: 'I am shy, that's why I am not getting into the crowd, not getting into people, not communicating with new people, not relating – because I am shy.' That shyness is just an explanation, a blanket explanation. It covers many things, but basically it covers the ego.

Silence

There are two kinds of silence: one you cultivate, one which arrives. The silence you cultivate is nothing but repressed noise. You can sit silently and if you sit long enough and you continue the practice for months and years, slowly you will become capable of repressing all noise. But still you will be sitting on a volcano which can erupt at any moment. Any excuse will do. This is not real silence, this is just imposed silence.

This is what is happening all around the world. People who try to meditate, who try to become silent, are only imposing silence upon themselves. Silence *can* be imposed; you can have a layer of silence around yourself, but it is just self-deception, that's all. That layer is not going to help you.

Real silence arises from your very being. It is not imposed from without, but comes from within. It rises from the centre and moves towards the circumference. It is a totally different phenomenon.

Simplicity

Simplicity is living without ideals. Ideals create complexity; they create division in you, hence complexity. The moment you are interested in becoming somebody else you become complex. If you are content with yourself as you are, that is simplicity.

The future brings complexity; being utterly in the present is simplicity.

Simplicity does not mean living a life of poverty. That is utterly stupid, because the person who imposes a life of poverty on himself is not simple at all. He is a hypocrite. The need to impose poverty means that deep down, you hanker for the diametrically opposite; otherwise why would there be any need to impose it? You impose a certain character upon yourself because you are just the opposite of it …

You cannot impose simplicity on yourself. That's why I never say that people like Mahatma Gandhi are simple. They are not, they cannot be. Simplicity is their ideal, they are trying to attain it, they are striving for it, they are straining for it, it is a great effort. How can you create simplicity out of effort? Effort means you are trying to improve upon existence. Existence is perfect as it is, it needs no improvement.

Simplicity simply means that which is. Simplicity means just being yourself, whoever you are, in tremendous acceptance, with no goals, no ideals.

Yet it needs guts to be simple. It needs guts because if you are simple you will never be adjusted to the so-called society around you. You will constantly be an outsider. But you will be utterly in harmony with yourself. There will be no conflict within you, no split within you. You will be simple, and simplicity has beauty.

Sleep

Buddha's chief disciple was Ananda, who lived with him for 40 years and served him with great love. He used to watch him all the time, in every possible way. He followed him like a shadow. And each of Buddha's movements was beautiful, graceful. Ananda also watched him when he was asleep, because he used to sleep in the same room in case the master needed him in the night. Awake or asleep, Buddha's grace was the same, his beauty was the same, his silence was the same.

One day Ananda said to him, 'I should not ask such questions, it looks so stupid, but I cannot contain my curiosity. I have watched you for hours when you are asleep. Sometimes in the middle of the night I wake up and watch you, sometimes just before you get up early in the morning I watch you, but it always seems to me that you are still awake even when you are asleep. You look so alive, so fresh! And one thing more – you never change your posture. You go to sleep and you wake up in the same posture. What is the secret of it?'

Buddha said, 'There is no secret. The body goes to sleep, but once you are awake you are awake! Day or night it makes no difference, the inner flame goes on burning. The body goes to sleep because the body gets tired, and now there is no mind any more, so no question of the mind arises at all.'

In the unenlightened person there is the body, the mind and the soul. And because of the mind the person cannot see the soul. The mind is a turmoil, a chaos; it is all smoke, it is all clouds. The enlightened person has no mind; there is only silence. So he has the body and he has the soul. The body tires, needs rest, but the soul is never tired, needs no rest; it is always awake. Once the mind is no longer there, then even in your sleep only the body sleeps, not you.

Smoking

If you want to stop smoking, don't stop right now – because that will not help and you will start again. But whenever you have an urge to smoke, first breathe deeply for five minutes. Start by exhaling. Exhale deeply. Inhale deeply and exhale deeply, but keep the emphasis more on the exhalation than on the inhalation. Squeeze your whole system so that all the air is out. Do this for five minutes before each cigarette …

And if after that five minutes your desire to smoke has disappeared, there is no need to smoke. If the desire remains, you can smoke.

Generally, say 75 times out of 100, the desire will disappear. That urge to smoke always comes when you are not enjoying life. If you are enjoying something you can forget cigarettes. If you are watching a movie and you are really into it, you will not smoke. If you are listening to music and you are really into it, you will not smoke. Whenever you are involved in something and are happy, you will not smoke. You will smoke only when you are not feeling in tune, so you want something to do. Good breathing will give you such a good feeling that you will not feel like smoking. You will feel so happy and so full of vitality, you will not feel like smoking.

In fact breathing does just the opposite to smoking, because through breathing you take in more oxygen. Your system functions on a higher plane, at a higher altitude, with more oxygen, and you feel more vital. Your blood circulates better and is purified better. Your whole system functions at the maximum level. With smoking you go on dumping carbon dioxide into your system and your system functions at the minimum level. Smoking is just the opposite of good breathing.

Snake

You must have seen the symbol – a very ancient symbol and a very significant one too – of a snake eating its own tail. Many ancient mystery schools used that symbol. The snake eating its own tail means a 180° turn. The snake has turned upon itself, consciousness has recoiled upon itself.

The snake has represented wisdom in almost all the cultures of the world. Jesus said, 'Be ye as wise as a snake.' And in the East the serpent symbolizes the inner energy of man, kundalini, which is why it is called 'serpent power'. The energy is coiled at the lowest centre of your being and when it uncoils, the snake starts rising upwards. All this shows that there is something in the snake which can be used as a metaphor.

The snake can catch hold of its own tail; the dog cannot do it. Dogs try – you must have seen them trying – and the more they try, the more they go crazy, because their tail goes on jumping with them. They think it is something separate and try to catch hold of it, but the more they try the more they are at a loss. Only the snake can catch its own tail, no other animal.

The same happens with enlightenment: your energy starts moving upon itself, it becomes a circle.

Society

Society is only a word – and a very dangerous word. Society is an illusion – only individuals exist. Ask the scientist, he will say there is no matter, only electrons. Matter is an illusion. In exactly the same way, those who understand human consciousness will say that society is an illusion. Electrons are true, so are individuals. But society is an illusion.

The belief that society exists has sabotaged every effort to change mankind. It is the reason why all our revolutions have failed. We have not yet listened to the Buddhas who have been telling of a totally different revolution: the revolution in the heart of the individual. The individual needs a mutation. If the individual can be helped, if the individual can be enlightened, if the individual can be persuaded to celebrate life, to enjoy life, then we will be able to change the social climate around the Earth.

But that is not the purpose of individual enlightenment, it is not a goal, it is just going to be a consequence.

Solitude

The lonely person is in a negative space. He is hankering for another. He is sad because he does not know how to enjoy being with himself, he does not know how to celebrate himself. All that he knows is relationship, so whenever he is in a relationship he feels at ease. Whenever he is with somebody he can forget himself.

To be with somebody is like alcohol, it is an intoxicant. It is simply drowning yourself, your worries, anxieties, your very existence in another person. And that person is doing the same with you. That's what people call relationship – each is using the other as a means to avoid the self.

Solitude is totally different. It is not loneliness, it is aloneness. It is not negative, it is utterly positive. It is not experiencing that another is absent but experiencing that you are present. It is so overwhelming an experience of your own presence that everything else fades from the mind and you start feeling ecstatic. The sheer joy of breathing, the sheer joy of being, the sheer joy of participating in existence is enough. It is a wonder to be, the wonder of wonders.

Then solitude becomes a temple. Blissfulness becomes the deity in it. And that's what meditation is all about: the art of changing loneliness into aloneness, into solitude.

Spirituality

One of the greatest misfortunes that has happened to humanity is that people are being told to be religious, not spiritual. Religion means the circumference and spirituality means the centre. Religion has something of spirituality, but only something – something like a reflection in a lake of a starry night, of a full moon. Spirituality is the real thing; religion is just a by-product.

But because people are told to be religious, they start decorating their circumference, they start cultivating character. Character is your circumference. But by painting your circumference, you are not changing your centre. But if you change the centre, the circumference automatically goes through a transformation.

Change the centre – that is spirituality. Spirituality is an inner revolution. It certainly affects your outer behaviour – because you are more alert, more aware, naturally your actions are different, your behaviour has a different quality, a different flavour, a different beauty – but this is only a by-product. Spirituality belongs to your essential being and religion only to the outermost: actions, behaviour, morality.

Religion is formal; going to the church every Sunday is a social affair. The church is nothing but a kind of club, one with religious pretensions. The spiritual person cannot belong to any church – Hindu, Christian, Mohammedan – it is impossible for him to belong to any. He follows no creed, no dogma.

Spirituality is one; religions are many. Spirituality is rebellion; religion is orthodoxy. Spirituality is individuality; religion is just remaining part of the crowd. Religion keeps you a sheep; spirituality is a lion's roar.

Spring
You can bring spring at any moment. Just give spring a call and let the sun and the wind and the rain enter into you …

Stress
A Canadian psychoanalyst, Dr Hans Selye, has spent his whole life working on one problem: stress. And he has come to some very profound conclusions. One is that stress is not always wrong; it can be used in beautiful ways. It is not necessarily negative, but if we think that it is negative, then we create problems.

Stress in itself can be used as a stepping-stone, it can become a creative force. But we have been taught down the ages that stress is bad, so that when you are under any kind of stress you become afraid. And your fear makes the situation even more stressful. The moment you feel under stress, you say, 'I have to relax.' Now, trying to relax will not help, because you cannot relax; in fact, trying to relax will create a new kind of stress. The stress is there and you are trying to relax and you cannot, so you are compounding the problem.

When you are under stress, use it as creative energy. First, accept it; there is no need to fight it. It is perfectly OK. Stress is simply an indication that the body is getting ready to fight something. So if you try to relax or take painkillers or tranquillizers, you are going against the body. The body is getting ready to do battle in a certain situation, to take up a certain challenge. Enjoy the challenge!

Even if sometimes you can't sleep at night there is no need to be worried. Use the energy that is coming up: walk up and down, go for a run, go for a long walk, work things out, plan what you want to do, what the mind wants to do. Rather than trying to go to sleep, which is not possible, use the situation in a creative way. It is simply telling you that the body is ready to fight the problem; this is no time to relax. You can relax later on.

In fact if you live your stress totally, you can only go so far, then the body automatically relaxes. If you try to relax in the middle of it, though, you create trouble for yourself. The body cannot relax in the middle. It is almost as if an Olympic runner is getting ready for a race. He is just waiting for the whistle and he will be off, he will go like the wind. He is full of stress; this is no time to relax. If he takes a tranquillizer he will never be of any use in the race. If he relaxes on the starting-line and tries to do TM he will certainly lose. His stress is gathering energy. He has to use it as energy, as fuel.

Selye has given this kind of stress a new name: he calls it 'eustress', like euphoria. It is a positive form of stress. When the runner has run his race he will fall into deep sleep and his stress will disappear of its own accord.

So try this too: when you are in a stressful situation, don't freak out, don't become afraid of it. Go into it, fight, do all that you can do, really get right into it. Use the stress to fight the problem. Allow it, accept it and welcome it. Stress is good, it prepares you to fight. You have tremendous energy and the more you use it, the more you have ...

And when you have worked it out, you will be surprised by how easy it is to relax. Maybe for two, three days you cannot sleep and then for 48 hours you can't wake up – and that is OK!

Success

Remember, if you think too much of success you will constantly be thinking of failure too. Success and failure cannot be separated. They come together in one package. So if you are thinking of success, somewhere deep down you will be afraid of failing. Who knows whether you are going to make it or not?

Success takes you into the future, gives you a greed game, an ego projection, ambition. And the fear also gives you a shaking, a trembling. The possibility of failure makes you waver. And with this wavering, with this greed, with this ambition, with all of this, your work will be in turmoil; you will be working here and looking there. You will be walking along a road and looking somewhere faraway in the sky. How can you possibly succeed?

Suchness

Try to understand the word 'suchness'. Buddha depends on that word very much. In Buddha's own language it is *tathata*. The whole of Buddhist meditation consists of living in this word, living with this word so deeply that the word disappears and you become the suchness. You eat in suchness, you sleep in suchness, you breathe in suchness, you love in suchness, you weep in suchness ... It becomes your style; you need not think about it, it is the way you are. You imbibe it, you digest it, it flows in your blood, it goes deep in your bones, it reaches the very beat of your heart.

Just remember suchness, not as a word but as a feeling. Then you will have no grudge, no complaint, no desire for things to be different. A tremendous acceptance will arise in you.

But remember, the word 'accept' is not very good. It is loaded – not because of the word itself, but because you tend to accept only when you feel helpless. You accept grudgingly, you accept halfheartedly. You accept a situation only when you cannot do anything about it. But deep down you still wish it were otherwise; you would have been happier if it had been otherwise. You accept like a beggar, not like a king – and the difference is great.

Suffering

Many people have the idea that you have to suffer if you are to grow. But growth in itself has no suffering in it; suffering comes from your resistance to growth. You create your suffering because you resist growth continuously, you don't allow it to happen. You are afraid to go with it completely; you go only halfheartedly. Hence the suffering – because you become divided, you become split. A part of you co-operates and a part of you resists. This conflict inside you creates suffering.

So drop the idea that you have to suffer to grow. It is sheer nonsense. If you co-operate totally with your growth, you will not suffer at all, you will rejoice. Every moment will be one of bliss and benediction.

So don't throw the responsibility for your suffering on growth. The mind is very tricky and cunning: it always throws the responsibility onto somebody or something; it never takes the responsibility itself. But the truth is that *you* are the cause of your suffering.

The real thing you are suffering from is your expectations. When they are not fulfilled – and they are never going to be fulfilled – frustration arises, failure arises, and you feel neglected, as if existence does not care for you.

Drop your expectations. Remain open, remain available to whatever happens, but don't plan ahead. Don't have any expectations for the future, don't have any fixed ideas about it, and much of your suffering will disappear.

Superman

Man is really only a bridge; man has no being. Man is a becoming, a process. He has to arrive; he is still on the way. Man has to surpass himself. He has to become a superman …

When you have reached your core, your very centre, when you have arrived at your deepest depth, when there is nowhere else to go, then you are no longer a man. Buddha is not a man; he is a superman. So is Jesus, so is Krishna, and so are all the awakened ones of the Earth. And you have to become part of those chains of awakened people: you have to become part of the glory that belongs to an awakened one. Each human being has to become a superman.

And this has nothing to do with race, blood. I am not using the word in the sense that Adolf Hitler used it. I am using it in a totally different sense, as the ultimate state of your awakening. Then how can you be called just a human being? You are superhuman. You have surpassed your humanity; you have gone beyond it. You have reached the other shore.

Sutras

In the East the greatest statements of the masters have been called sutras, threads, for a certain reason. We are born as a heap of flowers, just as a heap. Unless threads are run through the flowers, the heap will remain a heap and will never become a garland. And you can only be offered to God when you have become a garland, a harmony, a song. A heap is a chaos, a garland is a cosmos.

The sayings of the masters are called sutras, threads, because they can make a garland out of you.

Right now you are just gibberish. You can prove it. Sit in a room, close the door and start writing down whatever comes to mind. Don't edit anything, don't delete anything and don't add anything, because you are not going to show it to anybody. Keep a matchbox beside you so that once you have finished writing you can burn what you have written immediately. Just write whatever comes into your mind for 10 minutes. When you have finished, you will be surprised at what you have written. You will understand what I mean when I say that you are just gibberish.

It is really a great revelation to see how your mind goes on jumping from here to there, from one thing to another thing, accidentally, for no reason at all. What nonsensical thoughts go on running inside you, with no relevance, no consistency – just sheer wastage, a leakage of energy!

The sayings of the Buddhas are called sutras.

Tantra

When sex is just an unconscious, mechanical urge, it is wrong. Remember, sex itself is not wrong, it is the mechanicalness that is wrong. If you can bring some light of intelligence into your sexuality, that light will transform it. It will not be sexuality anymore – it will be something totally different, so different that you don't have a word for it.

In the East we have a word for it: *Tantra*. Tantra is the totally new energy created when sex becomes joined with intelligence. It is the capacity of expansion, that which goes on expanding. Sex shrinks you, Tantra expands you. It is the same energy, but it takes a turn. It is no longer selfish, no longer self-centred. It starts spreading – and carries on spreading to the whole of existence. With sex, you can attain orgasm for a moment and at a great cost. With Tantra you can live in the orgasm 24 hours a day, because your very energy becomes orgasmic. And your meeting is no longer with an individual person, your meeting is with the universe itself. You see a tree, you see a flower, you see a star and it is orgasmic. Your every movement is full of orgasmic peaks, and peaks upon peaks. And once you have experienced Tantra, sex disappears. Sex is a seed, Tantra is the tree.

Tea

You might have heard about Bodhidharma, one of the greatest masters of meditation in the whole history of humankind. A very beautiful story is told about him.

Bodhidharma was on a mountain in China and was concentrating on something outward. His eyes would blink and the concentration would be lost. So he tore off his eyelids, threw them away and went on concentrating. After a few weeks, he saw some plants growing on the spot where he had thrown his eyelids. Those plants became tea, from the mountain's name, Tah or Ta, and that is why tea helps you to stay awake. When your eyes are blinking and you are falling asleep, drink a cup of tea.

Zen monks consider tea to be sacred because it is Bodhidharma's eyelids. In Japan they have created beautiful ceremonies around tea drinking. Every house has a tearoom and the tea is served with religious ceremony. People will enter the tearoom as if they are entering a temple. Then the tea will be made, and everyone will sit silently listening to the samovar bubbling. There is the steam, the noise and everyone just listening. It is no ordinary thing … Tea has to be taken in a very meditative mood.

Teacher

The teacher is one who teaches borrowed knowledge. He knows nothing, he has not experienced anything, but he has heard it, read it. He is skilful in transmitting it verbally, intellectually. He is capable of communication.

The perfect teacher is one who knows that he does not know. The ordinary teacher tends to forget it. He starts believing in what he is teaching others. He is not only a deceiver, he is also deceived. He starts living in a deep auto-hypnotic sleep. First he convinces others and then, seeing their conviction, he becomes convinced himself.

Tears

People have almost lost the dimension of tears. They allow tears only when they are in deep pain or suffering. They have forgotten that tears can also be of happiness, tremendous delight, of celebration.

In fact tears have nothing to do with suffering or happiness. Tears have to do with anything that is inside and wants to overflow. It may be happiness, it may be unhappiness. Anything that is too intense, too unbearable, will overflow; the cup is too full. Tears come out of 'too-muchness'. So enjoy them.

Theology

I am reminded of Moses on Mount Sinai. He had gone there in search of God and he saw a very strange phenomenon which Jewish scholars are unable to explain because it looks fictitious: a fire, and within the fire a green bush, unburned. Moses could not believe his eyes. The flames were rising high and yet the bush inside the flames was green and its flowers were blooming as if a cool breeze were passing through, not a fire.

Attracted by this majestic sight, Moses went closer to the bush and suddenly he heard a voice: 'Moses, take your shoes off! You are on holy ground.' The voice was coming from the bush. As Moses went closer, leaving his shoes behind, he did not feel any heat; on the contrary, he felt very cool. And the dialogue that took place and culminated in the Ten Commandments was not with a person, but with an invisible voice coming from that green bush.

Theologians have been at work trying to figure it out. As far as I am concerned, I am not a theologian, but I can understand a little bit of poetry and I think it is a poetic statement, not a theological statement. Once you see it as a poetic statement all confusion disappears. What is being said is that life, or God, is a cool energy, so creative, so non-destructive, that even within its fire a bush will remain green and will grow and blossom.

Accept this life energy, which a great philosopher, Bergson, used to call *élan vital*. It is not something to be afraid of. If you communicate with it, enter into dialogue with it, you will be immensely enriched, not burned. For the first time your spring will come and your flowers will blossom.

Many ancient parables and stories are in fact poetic statements, but theologians have destroyed their beauty and their poetry by dragging them down and trying to prove that they are actual historical facts. They are not facts, they are far above facts; they are poetic realizations and poetic expressions.

Thinking

When you think, what happens? When you think, you are closed. The present world drops away from you and you move on a dream path in your mind. One word creates another, one thought creates another, and you go on moving from one to the next, moving further and further away from existence. Thinking is a means of going away. It is a dream way; it is dreaming in concepts.

Come back down to earth. Be very earthly in this sense; not worldly, but very earthly, substantial. Come back to existence.

Life's problems can be solved only when you become deeply rooted in existence. Flying in thoughts, you move away from your roots, and the further away you are, the less likely it is that you will solve anything. Rather, you will confuse everything and everything will become more entangled. And the more entangled things are, the more you will think, and the further away you will move ... Beware of thinking!

Time

In Sanskrit we have the same word for both 'time' and 'death': *kal.* Sanskrit may be the only language in the whole world that has the same word for time and death. That's why it can be said truthfully that it is the only language transformed by the insight of the seers. In the last 10,000 years thousands of people in the East have become enlightened and they have changed the very structure of the Sanskrit language. They have given it the colour of their enlightenment, they have made words luminous, they have given them new meanings which cannot be given by unenlightened persons.

Now to call time and death by the same name is a great insight. It is not a question of knowing linguistics, it is a question of experiencing something tremendously valuable.

Time and death are the same; to live in time means to live in death. And the moment time disappears, death disappears. So when you are utterly silent, when no thought moves in your mind, time disappears. You cannot have any idea what time it is. And the moment time disappears and the clock of your mind stops, suddenly you enter the world of the timeless, the eternal world, the world of the absolute.

In an incident that is not reported in the New Testament but it is part of the Sufi tradition, a seeker asks Jesus: 'What will be the most significant thing in your Kingdom of God?' And the answer is amazing. Jesus says: 'There shall be time no longer.' That will be the most significant thing in the Kingdom of God – there shall be time no longer. There will be no past, no future; there will be only the present.

And let me tell you that the present is not part of time. Of course in the schools, colleges and the universities you have been taught again and again that time has three tenses – past, present and future. That is absolutely wrong according to those who know. Past and future are time, but the present is not time. The present belongs to eternity. Past and future belong to this world of the relative, this world of change. Between the two penetrates the beyond, the transcendental, and that is the present. Now is part of eternity.

If you live in time, death is bound to happen. In fact, to say 'bound to happen' is not right – it is already happening. The moment a child is born he starts dying. It may take 70, 80 years, that's another matter. But however long it takes, the child dies – slowly, miserly, in instalments, a little bit every day, every hour – and goes on dying, dying, dying, until the process is complete. When you say that somebody has died today, don't be misguided by your statement. He has been dying for 80 years. Today the process is complete, that's all.

The source of time and death is the mind. The mind is time, the mind is death. One aspect of the mind is time, another aspect of the mind is death. But through meditation, through watching the mind, you can leave death behind.

The *Upanishads* call this process *neti neti,* neither this nor that. It is a process of elimination: 'I am not this – this body, this mind. Then who am I?' Eliminate the non-essential, put it aside, and go on eliminating the non-essential until only the essential is left.

And what is the essential? How will you decide that only the essential is left? When there is nothing left to be denied, nothing left to be eliminated. Go on emptying your house; throw all the furniture out. When there is nothing left to be thrown out, then a great revelation happens: You gain immortality; the absolute arises in you in all its beauty and splendour, in all its ecstasy.

Tomorrow

You don't have much time. Don't postpone anything. Don't say 'tomorrow' – tomorrow is a mirage. The moment is now. Be alert now, be awake now, this moment, and there is serenity and there is calmness. And suddenly you are relaxed. The source is contacted and you have arrived home. This is the home for which you have been searching for so many lives. But your methodology has been wrong. You have made it a goal. And it is not a goal, it is the source.

Totality

Just look at a child of three and you will see what liveliness should be. How joyous small children are, how sensitive to everything that is happening around them, how alert, watchful; nothing misses their eye. And how intense they are. If they are angry, they are just anger, pure anger. It is beautiful to see an angry child, because older people are always half-hearted; even if they are angry they are not totally in it, they are holding back. They don't do anything totally, they are always holding back, calculating. Their life has become lukewarm. It never gets to that intensity of 100°, where things evaporate, where something happens where revolution becomes possible.

But children always live at 100°, whatever they do. If they hate you, they hate you totally, and if they love you, they love you totally, and in a single moment they can change from one to the other. Children are so quick, they do not take their time, they do not brood over things. One moment they may be sitting in your lap and telling you how much they love you and the next they may jump out of your lap and say, 'I never want to see you again.' And you can see the totality of it in their eyes.

And because these feelings are total they do not leave a trace behind them. That's the beauty of totality: it does not accumulate psychological memory. Psychological memory is created only by partial living. Then everything that you have lived only in part hangs around you and this hangover continues for your whole life. Thousands of things are there, hanging unfinished.

That's the whole theory of karma – unfinished jobs, unfinished actions go on waiting to be finished, to be completed, and they go on goading you, 'Complete me!' because every action wants to be fulfilled.

But if you live totally, intensely, if you live the moment, then once it is finished you are free of it. You don't look back and you don't look ahead. You simply remain here now. There is no past, no future.

Tradition

The difference between science and religion is that science depends on tradition. Without a Newton, without an Edison, Albert Einstein could not have done his work at all. He needed a certain tradition; he could only stand on the shoulders of the past giants in the world of science.

So science needs a tradition, but religion does not. It is an individual experience, utterly individual. Once something is known in the world of science it need not be discovered again, it will be foolish to discover it again. You need not discover the theory of gravitation – Newton has done it. Now it is part of human tradition. It can be taught to any person who has a little bit of intelligence; even schoolchildren know about it.

But in religion you have to discover again and again. Buddha discovered, but that does not mean you can simply follow Buddha. Buddha was unique and you are unique, so the way Buddha has entered into truth is not going to help you. You are a different kind of house; the doors may be in different places. If you simply follow Buddha blindly, that very following will be misleading. Religious traditions cannot be followed. You can understand them, and understanding can be of immense help, but following and understanding are totally different things.

A religious tradition is nothing but footprints on the sands of time, footprints of enlightened people – but the footprints themselves are not enlightened. You can follow those footprints very religiously, but they will not lead you anywhere, because each person is unique. What happens when you follow a tradition? You become an imitator.

Tradition is of the past and enlightenment has to happen right now!

Transcendence

Transcendence precisely defines meditation. You have to transcend three things and then the fourth is achieved. The fourth is your true nature. Gurdjieff used to call his way 'the fourth way' and in the East we call the ultimate state of being *turiya,* the fourth.

The first thing you have to transcend is the body. You have to become aware that you are in the body, but you are not it. The body is beautiful, you have to take care of it, you have to be very loving towards it. It is serving you beautifully. You don't have to be antagonistic towards it. Religions have been teaching people to be antagonistic towards their body, to torture it – they call it asceticism. That is sheer stupidity! And they think that by torturing the body they will be able to transcend it. They are utterly wrong. The only way to transcend something is through awareness, not torture. There is no question of torturing. You don't torture your house; you live in it, but you know that you are not it. It is the same with your body – there is no need to go on a fast, there is no need to stand on your head, there is no need to contort your body in a thousand and one postures. Just watching, becoming aware, is enough. And the same is the key for the other two forms of transcendence.

The second thing you have to transcend is the mind. That is a second concentric circle. The body is the first, the outermost. The mind is closer to your being than the body. The body is the gross, the mind is the subtle, and then there is a third circle, the subtlest and closest: your heart – the world of your feelings, emotions, moods. You have to transcend that too. But the key is the same.

Start with the body, though, because the body is the most easily observable thing. It is an object. Thoughts are also objects, but they are less visible. Once you have become aware of the body you will be able to watch your thoughts too. And once you have become aware of your thoughts you will be able to watch your moods too, but they are the subtlest, so do that last.

Once you become aware of these three concentric circles around your centre and you transcend them, the fourth state will happen of its own accord. Suddenly you will know who you are. You won't know verbally – you won't be told, you won't get an answer, you won't be able to tell anybody about it in words – but you will know. You will know in the same way that you know when you have a headache. You will know in the same way that you know when you are hungry or thirsty. You will know in the same way that you know that you have fallen in love. You cannot prove it, there is no way to prove it, but you know. And that knowing is self-evident; it is undeniable.

When you have reached this fourth state, you have transcended the world.

I don't teach renunciation of the world. I teach transcendence of the world – and this is the way.

Transcendental Meditation

Transcendental Meditation and similar methods have become more important in the West recently for the simple reason that the West is losing the art of how to fall asleep. People are suffering from sleeplessness more and more; they have to depend on tranquillizers. Transcendental Meditation is a non-medicinal tranquillizer. And nothing is wrong if you know that you are using it as a tranquillizer, but if you think that you are doing something religious then you are stupid. If you think Transcendental Meditation is going to lead you to meditation you are a fool, an utter fool, just a simpleton.

Transcendental Meditation is not going to lead you into meditation because meditation means awareness. TM takes you towards just the opposite of awareness: it takes you towards sleep. I am not against sleep – it is a healthy thing and I prescribe TM for all those who suffer from sleeplessness – but remember that sleep has nothing spiritual about it. It is good for the body and it is good for the mind too, but it has nothing to do with the spiritual dimension. The spiritual dimension opens up only when you are awake, fully awake. And the only way to be awake is to drop all sleep and all dreaming.

Transformation

The greatest desire in the world is for inner transformation. The desire for money is nothing, the desire for power, prestige, is nothing. The greatest desire is the so-called spiritual desire. And once you are caught in that desire you will remain miserable forever.

Transformation is possible, but not by desiring it. Transformation is possible only by relaxing into that which is, whatever it is. Unconditional acceptance brings transformation.

Trust

Trust is a mystery – that is the first thing to remember about trust. So it cannot be explained. But I can give you a few indications of it, a few hints, just fingers pointing at the moon …

Trust is the highest form of love, it is the essential core of love. Love itself is a mystery and indefinable, but it is like a circumference and trust is its very centre, its very soul. Love is like a temple and trust is the innermost shrine.

Ordinarily people think that trust means faith; that is wrong. Trust does not mean faith. Faith is emotional, sentimental. Faith creates fanatics. Trust creates only a quality of religiousness. Faith is borrowed – borrowed from your parents or from the society in which you are born. It is a bondage, because you have been forced into it by subtle strategies. Faith is accidental. People live in faith out of fear or out of greed, but not out of love. Trust comes out of love.

It is your own growth that brings you to trust; it is your own experience, it is your own knowing. Faith happens through conditioning and trust happens through deconditioning. You have to drop faith before you can trust.

And the third thing to remember about trust is that it is not belief either. Belief is a trick of the mind to repress doubt. We are born with many doubts, millions of doubts, and doubt is natural, it is a gift of nature, but it creates trouble for us. Doubt is a sword – it cuts through all beliefs, it is dangerous.

Truth is the ultimate peak, but the higher you climb, the more dangerous the path. A single wrong step and you will be lost forever. If you doubt and go on doubting, a moment comes when all that you have ever believed disappears, evaporates. It is almost a state of madness. You can fall any moment into the abyss that surrounds you. If you fall, it is a breakdown. If you remain alert and aware, watchful, cautious, then it is a breakthrough.

Trust is the ultimate breakthrough. It helps you to know the truth on your own. And truth liberates only when it is your truth; no one else's truth can liberate you.

Truth

Truth is beyond structure. It comes only when you are in an unstructured state of consciousness. It comes only when there is no expectation of it, no preparation for it, because all preparation is expectation. Truth comes unawares, truth comes as a surprise. You cannot manage and manufacture it; it comes when it comes.

There is no path to truth. This is one of the most fundamental things to understand. If you are searching for truth, all paths will lead you astray, because following a path means that you have already decided what truth is. You have decided the direction, the dimension, you have decided how to approach it, what discipline to follow, what doctrine to adopt. Your destination will just be a projection of your own mind. It will be just your own mind playing a game with itself. There is no way to truth, because the mind is the barrier and it is the mind that creates the way. The mind has to go. The mind has to cease for truth to be.

Truth is not a discipline either, because truth is freedom. Truth is a bird on the wing, not a bird in the cage. The cage may be of gold, may be studded with diamonds, but a cage is a cage and it cannot contain freedom. Truth can never be a prisoner, its intrinsic quality is freedom, so only those who are capable of being free will reach it.

Unawareness

People are moving unconsciously, mechanically. They are unaware; they don't know what they are doing. How can they know what they are doing? They don't even know who they are.

If you don't know your being, you can't be aware of your doing. It is impossible. First you have to be aware of being – and that is growth. Growing inwards is growth, reaching inwards is growth.

Unconsciousness

There is no evil, hence there is no need to be delivered from anything. There is only one thing and that is a state of unconsciousness, unknowing, unawareness. I will not call it evil – it is a situation, a challenge, an adventure, it is not evil. Existence is not evil, existence is an opportunity to grow. And, of course, the opportunity to grow is possible only if you are tempted in thousands of ways, if you are called forth by unknown aspirations, if a tremendous desire arises in you to explore … And the only thing that can prevent you is unconsciousness, unawareness.

Understanding

Understanding is totally different from knowledge. Knowledge is borrowed, understanding is your own. Knowledge comes from without, understanding wells up from within. Knowledge is ugly, because it is secondhand. And knowledge can never become part of your being. It will remain alien, it will remain foreign, it cannot put down roots inside you.

Understanding grows out of you, it is your own flowering. It is authentically yours; so it has beauty, and it liberates.

Unhappiness

Happiness is when you disappear. Unhappiness is when there is too much of you. You are the discord, your absence will be the accord.

Sometimes you have glimpses of happiness when by some accident you are not there. When you are looking at nature, or looking at the stars, or holding the hand of your beloved, or making love, sometimes you are not there. If you are there, there will be no happiness in what you are doing. If you are making love to your beloved and it is really as you express it, a 'making', then there will be no happiness in it. Love cannot be made. You can be in it or not in it, but there is no way to make it. The English expression is ugly. To 'make love' is absurd. How can you make it? If the maker is there, the doer is there, the technician goes on existing. And if you are following a technique from Masters and Johnson or Vatasyayana or some other source, and you are not lost in it, there will be no happiness in it. When you are lost in it, when you are possessed by the whole, when the part is not separate from the whole, that is an orgasmic experience. That is what happiness is.

Uniqueness

I do not believe in equality for the simple reason that it is impossible. Socrates is Socrates, and you cannot create four billion Socrates to make the whole world equal.

Just like Socrates, every human being is unique. No two human beings can be equal, and they should not be, otherwise the world will become boring. Imagine roses and roses all over the world, the same colour, the same size ... No. The world needs all kinds of flowers, all colours; that gives it richness.

I believe in the uniqueness of the individual, I don't believe in the equality of the individual. But I do believe in equal opportunity for everybody. That is a totally different thing – equal opportunity for the rose to grow, equal opportunity for the lotus to grow, equal opportunity for the marigold to grow. Somebody wants to become a painter, and somebody else a doctor, and somebody else a sculptor – and they should be given equal opportunities. But they should not be forced to be equal – that will be murdering the whole richness of humanity.

Equal opportunity for everybody to be unequal, unique.

Unknowable

These three words have to be remembered: the known, the knowable and the unknowable.

The known was unknown yesterday. The knowable is unknown today but tomorrow it may become knowable, known. Science believes a moment will come in history, some time in the future, where there will be nothing left to know, when the whole unknown will have become known. Science believes in only two categories, the known and the unknown. But religion has a third category: the unknowable, which always remains unknowable. It was unknowable yesterday, it is unknowable today, it will remain unknowable tomorrow. That unknowable will always remain a mystery.

And that unknowable is called God, truth, nirvana, *tao, dharma, logos*. So many names have been given to it, but one quality is definitely there in all these words: absolute mystery. You can enter into it, you can become part of it but you cannot know it. You can live it but you cannot know it, you can taste it but you cannot say anything about it, You can feel it in your belly, but you will be absolutely dumb. And that is the most precious experience. It is experienceable but not expressible. That's why it cannot become part of the known.

Many people have experienced it – Buddha, Lao Tzu, Patanjali, Kabir – but nobody has ever been able to say anything about it. Lao Tzu begins his book *Tao Te Ching*: 'Truth is that which cannot be expressed.' All that those who have experienced it can say is how to find it, how to seek it.

That is our search – for the unknowable.

Unpredictable

Predictions are possible only about things, not about consciousness. Consciousness is unpredictable. What is going to blossom in you can be known only when it blossoms.

Vacillation

Millions of people are fence-sitters, vacillating this way or that. Why do people vacillate so much? Because from early childhood they are told not to commit any mistakes. That is one of the greatest teachings of all the societies all over the world – and it is very dangerous, very harmful.

If you really want to grow, mature, if you really want to know what this life is all about, don't vacillate. Involve yourself with life, get committed to life, don't remain a spectator. Don't go on thinking, 'Should I do this or that?' You can go on vacillating your whole life, and the more you vacillate, the more trained you become in vacillation.

Life is for those who know how to commit – how to say 'yes' to something, how to say 'no' to something decisively, categorically. Once you have categorically said 'yes' or 'no' to something, then you can jump into it, then you can dive deep into the ocean.

Even if sometimes you commit to the wrong thing, even then it is good to commit, because the day you know it is wrong you can get out of it. The very least you will have learned is never to get into anything like that again. It will have been a great experience; it will have brought you closer to truth. So my own suggestion is to teach children to commit as many mistakes as possible, with only one condition: don't commit the same mistake twice. And they will grow, and they will experience more and more, and they will not vacillate.

Vertical

Time consists of two tenses, not three. The present is not part of time; the past is time, the future is time. The present is the penetration of the beyond into the world of time.

You can think of time as a horizontal line. A is followed by B, B is followed by C, C is followed by D, and so on and so forth; it is a linear progression. Existence is not horizontal, existence is vertical. Existence does not move in a line from A to B and from B to C, existence moves in intensity, from A to a deeper A, from the deeper A to an even deeper A. It is diving into the moment. Existence is vertical.

Victory

In Japan, when wrestlers fight, first they will bow down to each other. This ritual is very symbolic. The Zen explanation is that whether you are defeated or victorious does not matter, you need each other, you depend on each other. If you are defeated and your opponent is victorious, he has to bow down to you because without you he could not have been victorious. His victory depends on your defeat and he has to be thankful for that. He cannot be victorious alone. So even victory does not create an ego trip. And if you are defeated and you know it is just a game and that you were a part of it, there is nothing to be worried about. No problem arises.

In Mexico the ancient tradition is that the father has to give rewards, toys, to every child irrespective of success or failure. The child who has come first in the class gets a reward and the one who has failed also gets one. And there is no difference – it is irrelevant. That's a tremendous insight: it doesn't matter whether you fail or you succeed in life, it's all a game. You are rewarded all the same.

And psychologists who have been studying this have come to feel that Mexican children are more at ease with life – less worried, more relaxed. Most children become very tense very early on – at five years old, six years old. They are tense and worried about whether they are going to make it or not. Our system destroys childhood and creates the poison of ambition. If a child comes first it is something great, if he comes second he has not been up to the mark and he will carry that wound always and when he comes home a failure, nobody will even look at him, except to condemn him. We make things unnecessarily serious. Our children carry the whole burden of the Earth.

Violence

We have worked for thousands of years to make the Earth a big madhouse, and we have succeeded. There is violence everywhere for the simple reason that we have, in subtle ways, not allowed people's energies to be creative. And whenever creative energies are thwarted, they become destructive.

Violence is not the real problem. The real problem is how to help people to be creative. A creative person cannot be violent because his energies are moving in the direction of godliness. We call God the creator. Whenever you are creating something you participate in godliness. But for thousands of years we have destroyed every possible door to creativity. Instead of helping people to be creative, we train them to be destructive. We have respected the warrior, the soldier, too much.

We need lovers, not fighters. But love is condemned and violence is praised. It is easier to fight with a person and decide who is right. 'Might is right.' That rule still remains – the rule of the jungle.

Civilization is only an idea which has not yet been realized. We are just superficially civilized. It's not even skin deep. Just scratch a little and you will find the animal coming out – a ferocious animal, far more ferocious than any wild animal because wild animals, however wild they are, don't carry bombs, atom bombs, hydrogen bombs. Compared to man and his violence, all animals are left far behind.

Virginity

'Virgin' simply means utterly pure, so pure that there is no sexuality in the mind. It is not a question of the body, but a question of the mind. And at the deepest core everybody is a virgin. Virginity means a purity of love.

Now 'virgin birth' has nothing to do with biological virginity; that is utter nonsense. Jesus is not born of a biologically virgin mother. But Jesus must have been born out of great love. Love is always virgin. Love transcends sex – that is the meaning of virginity.

But there are foolish people everywhere; they go on insisting that Jesus was born of a virgin mother. They make him a laughing stock. And because of their foolishness, a great parable, a great metaphor, loses all meaning.

Virtue

Real virtue has nothing to do with so-called morality. There is one very profound and pregnant statement of Socrates: 'Knowledge is virtue.' By 'knowledge' he means wisdom, knowing, because his whole emphasis was 'Know thyself.' That's what I mean by being conscious, because it is only consciousness that makes you capable of knowing yourself. And the moment you have known yourself you cannot do anything harmful to anybody. It is simply impossible. You cannot be destructive.

It is like a man who has eyes. How can you think that he will try to walk through the wall? He has eyes so he knows where the door is. He will walk through the door. But the blind man will knock on the walls and even try to get out through the wall or through a window. He does not know where the door is. He will ask others where the door is. But each moment you are in a different house – as far as life is concerned – and each moment the house is changing. Sometimes the door is on the right and sometimes it is on the left, and sometimes it is at the back and sometimes at the front. So no directions from others can be of much help. You need your own eyes. Then there is no need to ask, then there is no need to think about the door. Whenever you want to get out, you simply look and you know where the door is.

That's what consciousness gives you: an insight, a new vision, a way of seeing, a new eye. In the East we call it the third eye. That is only a metaphor, but there are a few fools who try to dissect dead bodies to find out where the third eye is. They have not understood the metaphor, they have not understood the poetry of the words. The third eye does not exist in the physical body, it is only a way of saying that you have found how to see directly into reality, that you have become conscious. And out of that consciousness comes virtue.

And remember, if virtue is imposed from the outside, then it is regimentation. When it comes from the within it has an individuality. It is not like ready-made clothes, it is tailor-made for you, it is made by your consciousness. It is in total harmony with your being.

And this is my insistence, that you find your own morality, your own virtue. Then your virtue has your signature. Then it is alive, breathing, and then you are doing it not for any other reason other than it's the right thing to do. Your very heart wants to do it. Then you are not asking for any rewards in heaven, you are not greedy for anything and you are not afraid of hell, of any punishment. You are doing exactly what your insight is telling you to do, whatever the result, whatever the ultimate consequence.

Nobody of deep consciousness ever cares about consequences. They act immediately, respond to reality directly – and that's all. And they enjoy the moment when they act with reality, with their total being. They enjoy that harmony, that meeting, that merger, that union.

Voice, Inner

There are many people here who go on listening to inner voices. These inner voices are just crap. These are just fragments of your mind; they have no value at all. And sometimes you may think that you are listening to an inner guide or a master from the beyond or a spirit, and you can go on imagining these things. But you will be simply fooling yourself.

These voices are all fragments of your mind. And if you go on following them you will go crazy, because one part will pull you to the north, another part to the south. You will start falling apart. Remember, this is a neurosis. You have to learn to watch all these voices. Don't trust any of them. Only trust silence. Don't trust any voice, because all voices are from the mind. And you don't have one mind, you have many.

We think we only have one mind. That fallacy persists. But we have many minds. In the morning, one mind is on top. By noon, another mind is on top. By the evening, a third mind ... Gurdjieff used to say that you have many selves, Mahavira has said that man is poly-psychic. It's true – you are a crowd! And if you go on listening to these voices and following them you will be simply destroying your whole life.

Vows

Life is never changed by vows, life is changed by awareness. Never take a vow; a vow simply means that you are forcing something upon yourself.

Instead, try to understand. When there is understanding there is no need to take a vow; understanding is enough. You understand something is wrong and drop it. Understanding is enough; no other discipline is ever needed. Whenever you need some other discipline it means something is missing in your understanding.

Vulnerability

Bliss is a rain shower. When it really happens it is almost like rain – you are soaked in it, bathed in it. And all that is needed for it to happen is just vulnerability; nothing else is required. Don't protect yourself against it, that's all.

Waiting

Waiting has to be pure. Enjoy waiting for its own sake. Don't you see the beauty of just waiting – the purity of it, the benediction of it, the innocence of it? Just waiting, not even knowing what you are waiting for …

See the point of it – pure waiting, not knowing what is going to happen. If you know what is going to happen, that will have been supplied by your past. It will be a continuity with the past; it will not be new. It may be modified, but it will be the same thing, it will be a repetition.

How can you know what is going to happen? You have not known it before, so how can you even imagine it?

Finding that there is no way to imagine the future, no way to imagine the unknown, the known ceases. All ideas disappear – ideas about God, ideas about *samadhi,* enlightenment, they all disappear. In that disappearance is enlightenment.

Never think for a single moment that your idea of enlightenment is going to be fulfilled. How can you have any idea of enlightenment? Whatever idea you have is going to be wrong.

When enlightenment happens you will be surprised. You read all the scriptures and it wasn't mentioned anywhere. It can't be mentioned. When you arrive at the reality of it, when it explodes in you, then you will know that no Buddha has ever been able to describe it. Millions of Buddhas have talked about it, but you know that nobody has ever been able to describe it. And that is good, because otherwise it would never be a new phenomenon to anybody.

But one thing is certain: the waiting is infinitely beautiful, the waiting is infinitely joyous.

Waking Up

You can wake up. It is only a question of remembering that you can wake up. Nothing else is needed, no other effort, no method, no technique, no path. Just a remembrance that, 'This is my dream.' A remembrance that, 'I have decided to dream it – and the moment I decide not to dream it, I will be awake.' Once your co-operation is withdrawn, the dream is nullified.

If you are living in misery, you are creating it. And nobody else can take it away from you unless you decide not to create it any more. Your hell is your work. All that you are is your creation. In a single moment, you can wake up.

War

We have lived with the calamity of war too long. We have to destroy all the gods of war and in their place we have to create a temple of love. We should kill all the gods of war, because only through their death will the god of love be born.

War exists not because there are warring groups outside in the world; fundamentally war exists because we are in conflict within ourselves. The root of war is within; on the outside you only see the branches and the foliage of it. After every 10 years, humanity needs a great world war. In 10 years, we accumulate so much rage, madness, insanity inside ourselves that it has to erupt.

Unless we transform the very script, unless we give ourselves a totally new programme of living and being, we can go on talking about peace but we will go on preparing for war. That's what we have been doing for thousands of years: talking of peace and creating war. The absurdity is that we have been fighting even in the name of peace! The greatest wars have been fought in the name of peace. Our past has been utterly destructive. With the same energy, we could have created paradise on Earth, and all that we have done is to create a hell instead.

It is not a question of changing the political ideologies of the world, it is not a question of teaching people to be brotherly, because these things have been done and they have all failed. Something more basic is wrong. We are split, and the same people who talk about peace are the cause of the split. The politician creates war without, and the priest creates war within. This is the longest and the greatest conspiracy against humanity. They have divided the human being into good and bad, lower and higher, the earthly and the divine, the material and the spiritual. They have created a rift inside the human soul; that's why there is a constant internal war. Everybody is fighting themselves and when it becomes too much they start fighting somebody else.

That's why in times of war, people look happier. Their faces shine with enthusiasm, their step has rhythm and purpose. They are thrilled, because at least for a few days they will not need to fight with themselves; they have found a scapegoat outside. It may be the fascist, it may be the communist, it may be the Mohammedan, it may be the Christian – it doesn't matter, as long as somebody is there outside it is an escape from the inner fight. In a very sick way it is relaxing. But an outer war cannot go on forever; sooner or later we have to turn inwards again.

My vision is of an integrated soul. The body is respected, not denied; it is loved, praised, we are grateful for it. Matter is not condemned, it is enjoyed; it is part of our spiritual growth. There is no duality: it is a dialectic of growth. This is how we move – on two feet. The bird flies on two wings. Matter and spirit, body and soul, lower and higher, are two wings.

What I am trying to bring is something utterly new, something that has never existed before on Earth: a human being who is at ease with both the worlds, this and that, a human being who is as worldly as one can be and as otherworldly as one can be, a human being who is a great synthesis, a human being who is not schizophrenic, a human being who is whole and holy.

Watching

Real silence happens when you start watching the noise of your mind. There is a constant traffic in the mind – thoughts, memories, imagination, thousands of desires. It is always a crowd moving in all directions. If you can stand by the side of the road and just watch, without any evaluation or judgement, without condemning anything or appreciating anything, if you can just sit on the bank of the river, watching the flow of the river, unconcerned, detached, just being a pure witness, then the miracle will happen.

I am not telling you to do anything. Meditation is not doing anything at all, it is pure awareness. Just go on watching and tremendous and incredible things will start happening. A miracle will happen, the greatest miracle in life. Your body will become graceful, light, unburdened; you will see great weights, mountainous weights, falling from your body. Your body will start purifying itself of all kinds of toxins and poisons. You will see your mind is not as active as before; its activity will become less and less and gaps will arise, gaps in which there are no thoughts. Those gaps are the most beautiful experiences, because through those gaps you start seeing things as they are without any interference of the mind.

Slowly, slowly, your moods will start disappearing. You will no longer be very joyous and no longer very sad. The difference between joy and sadness will become less. Soon a moment of equilibrium will be reached when you are neither sad nor joyous. And that is the moment when bliss is felt. That tranquillity, that silence, that balance, is bliss.

Now there are no more peaks and no more valleys, no more dark nights and no more moonlit nights. All those polarities disappear. You settle exactly in the middle.

And all these miracles go on becoming deeper and deeper, and ultimately, when your body is in total balance, your mind is absolutely silent and your heart is no longer full of desires, a quantum leap happens in you. Suddenly you become aware of the fourth – a state you have never been aware of before. And that is you, the fourth. You can call it 'the soul', 'the self', 'God' or whatever you want to call it, that is up to you; any name will do because it has no name of its own.

Water

In all the primitive tribes water symbolizes life. Life is based on water, the human body is 85 per cent water. And the life of animals and trees and man and birds, all life depends on water. So water was one of the basic elements to be worshipped. Just as the sun was worshipped by all primitive people, so water was also worshipped; both were respected as gods. And water is significant as a metaphor also.

Water represents a few things. One: it has no form, yet it can take any form, it is capable of adjusting into any form. You pour it into a pot, it takes the form of the pot; you pour it into a glass, it takes the form of the glass. It is infinitely adjustable. That's its beauty: it knows no rigidity. And we should be unrigid, unfrozen, like water, not like ice.

Two: water is always moving towards the sea. Wherever it is, its movement is always towards the sea, towards the infinite. We should be like water, always moving towards godliness. Water remains pure if it moves and flows; it becomes impure, stagnant, if it becomes dormant. We should be always flowing, moving, never getting stuck anywhere. It is by getting stuck that we become dirty, impure. If we are ready to move from one moment to another moment without any hang-ups, without carrying the load of the past, we will remain innocent, pure.

Wholeness

Respect yourself, love yourself, because there has never been a person like you and there never will be again. Existence never repeats itself. You are utterly unique, incomparably unique. You need not be like somebody else, you need not be an imitator. You have to be authentically yourself, your own being. You have to do your own thing.

The moment you start accepting and respecting yourself you start becoming whole. Then there is nothing to divide you, then there is nothing to create a split …

Your body is your temple, it is sacred. Your body is not your enemy. It is not irreligious to love your body, to take care of your body. It is religious. It is irreligious to torture your body and to destroy it. The religious person will love his body because it is the temple where the divine lives.

You and your body are not really two, but the manifestation of one. Your soul is your invisible body and your body is your visible soul. I teach this unity, and with this unity, man becomes whole. I teach joy, not sadness. I teach playfulness, not seriousness. I teach love and laughter, because to me there is nothing more sacred than love and laughter, and there is nothing more prayerful than playfulness. I teach the flowering of a new humanity, which will not think of the future and which will not live with shoulds and oughts, which will not deny any natural instinct, which will accept the body, which will accept all that is given by existence with deep gratitude.

Yes, my approach to life is holistic, because to me, to be whole is to be holy.

Why

'Why?' is the wrong question to ask. Things simply are. There is no reason for them, no reason why. The question 'Why?', once accepted, will lead you further and further into philosophy, and philosophy is a wasteland. You will not find any oasis there, it is a desert. Ask 'Why?' and you have started moving in the wrong direction; you will never come home.

'Why?' is a mind question. The question comes from the mind, the answers will come from the mind, and the mind is capable of turning each answer into a new question. You will be moving in a vicious circle. To ask the question 'Why?' is to fall into the trap of the mind.

Existence is, there is no reason for it. That's what we mean when we say it is a mystery. It should not be there and it is. There seems to be no need for it to be there, no reason for it to be there, and it is there. That's all.

Wife

I don't know much about wives. I am an unmarried man. But I have observed many wives and many husbands. So this is not my experience, just my opinion!

There are two things necessary to keep your wife happy. First, let her think she is having her own way. And second, let her have it.

Wisdom

It is possible to have knowledge but not wisdom. You can have as much knowledge as you want. It is easy, you just need a little mental effort, a little exertion. You can go on and on feeding your memory system. It is a computer; you can accumulate whole libraries in it. But wisdom is not something that you can accumulate, because it does not arise through the mind at all. It arises through the heart, through love, not through logic.

When the heart is open with love, with trust, when the heart has surrendered to the whole, then a new kind of insight arises in you – a clarity, a tremendously deep understanding of what life is all about, of who you are, of why this whole existence exists in the first place. All the secrets are

197

revealed, but through love not through logic, through the heart not through the head. Existence has a direct connection with the heart, but no connection with the head at all. So if you want to approach reality, approach through the heart.

Once you have known wisdom through the heart then you can use your mind too, as a good servant. You can even use the knowledge accumulated by the mind in the service of wisdom – but not before you have known wisdom through the heart.

So, don't waste time in accumulating unnecessary information. People go on accumulating such stupid information, it is utterly ridiculous. Children are forced to remember the names of kings and queens and their birth date and their death date – and what do they have to do with the poor child?

Once a teacher asked a child, 'If Adam had never left the Garden of Eden what would have happened?'

The child said, 'One thing is certain: there would have been no history and no history class! It all began with Adam getting out of the Garden of Eden.'

Knowledge brings information; wisdom brings transformation.

Within

It is one of the greatest mysteries of life that we are born with perfect bliss in our being and we remain beggars because we never look into ourselves. We take ourselves for granted, as if we already know all that is within. That is a very idiotic idea, but it prevails all over the world. We are ready to go to the moon to search for bliss, but we are not ready to go inside ourselves for the simple reason that we already think we know. And we don't know ourselves at all.

Socrates is right when he says, 'Know thyself.' In those two words the whole wisdom of all the sages is condensed, because in knowing thyself all is known and all is fulfilled and all is achieved.

We don't have to become perfect – we are born perfect. And we don't have to invent bliss, we only have to discover it. It is not such a difficult matter as people think; it is a very simple process of relaxing, resting and slowly getting centred.

The day you stumble upon your centre, suddenly there is light all around; you have found the switch. It is just like groping in a dark room – you go on groping and then you find the switch and light is all around. But you can sit in darkness for the whole night, crying and weeping just underneath the light switch. And that's actually the situation; we are crying and weeping unnecessarily.

So those who have known have a very strange feeling about people. They feel great compassion but they laugh too. They can see the absurdity of it all – that you have it already but you are running hither and thither for no reason at all. And because of your running, you go on missing it. And they have great compassion also, because you are suffering – that is true, although your suffering is simply foolish.

This absurd, ridiculous life pattern has to be changed completely. Look within, and if you cannot find anything there, then look outside. But I say categorically that if you look within you will find it – find the Kingdom of God, the perfect bliss, the absolute truth. Nobody is an exception, it is an absolute law. Look within and you will find it. And with it comes freedom and great fragrance. Life becomes a dance, a poem, a constant ecstasy; moment to moment it goes on growing.

Witnessing

In witnessing, the mind is only a bio-computer, a mechanism, separate from you; you are no longer identified with it. When you want to retrieve a memory you can use the mind to play it back just as you would use a tape recorder. The mind is really a tape recorder. But it is not switched on all the time. When necessary, the witness – the person of meditation, of awareness – is capable of switching the mind on or off.

If I am talking to you, for example, I have to switch the mind on; otherwise language will not be possible. No-mind is silent, there is no language; only the mind can supply language, so I have to use the mind to relate to your mind. When I go back and sit in my room, I switch the mind off. In my room I don't need it.

When you are witnessing, you are the watcher and the mind is the watched. It is a beautiful mechanism, one of the most beautiful mechanisms that nature has given to you. So you can use it when needed for factual memory – for phone numbers, for addresses, for names, for faces ... It is a good tool, but that's all it is.

Womb

Some people never come out of the womb. Even when they are dying, their need for others, their need for contact, relationship, continues. They have never come out of the womb. They may have come out physically 90 years ago, but if they have always been seeking for relationship, always been greedy for bodily contact, they have never emerged. They have been living in a lost womb again and again in their dreams.

It is said that whenever a man falls in love with a woman, he is falling back into the womb. And it may be, it is almost certain – I say 'may be' because it is not yet a scientifically proved hypothesis – that the urge to enter the woman's body, the sexual urge, may be nothing but a substitute for entering the womb again. All sexuality may be a search for how to enter the womb again. And whenever you are lying with a woman, curled up, you feel good. Every man, however old, becomes a child again and every woman, however young, becomes a mother again. In love the woman starts playing the role of the mother and the man starts playing the role of the baby. Even a young woman becomes a mother and even an old man becomes a child.

And psychologists say that all the ways that man has invented to make himself comfortable are just ways of creating a womb outside. Look at a comfortable room: if it is really comfortable it must have something in common with the womb – the warmth, the cosiness, the silk, the velvet, the inner touch of the mother's skin. The pillows, the bed – everything that gives you a feeling of comfort is somehow related to the womb. All comfort is, deep down, womblike.

Work

Once a man came to see me. He was a bus driver. Of course driving a bus in a city like Bombay or Delhi will bring you to the edge of a nervous breakdown. The bus driver was very nervous, shaking.

He told me, 'I want to get rid of this job, it is too much! I cannot sleep – it is giving me nightmares. All day at the wheel in such neurotic traffic, I cannot relax for a single moment.'

I told him, 'Try a meditation that I will give you, for seven days. Take it as a challenge that these people are running into the middle of the road and that everything is in disorder. Take it that they are just creating a situation to test your skill. Take it as a game. Take it as a situation in which your energy is put to the test and your skill is being judged.'

This idea appealed to him and after seven days he came back and said, 'It has worked … Tremendous! Now I am not worrying about the road, I am enjoying it! The more disorderly it is, the more I enjoy it. It is really beautiful how I can avoid all the traffic problems. When I go back home, I am almost like a victorious athlete, like somebody who has won a gold medal at the Olympics!'

Take work as a game and enjoy it. Everything is a challenge.

World

I declare to you that this is the only world there is and this is the only life there is. Don't start thinking of some other life somewhere after death, beyond the seven skies, in heaven. Those are all just mind dreams, mind trips, new ways to fall asleep again.

Hence my insistence that no seeker has to leave the world, because leaving the world is part of a dream of reaching another world. And because there is no other world, all your efforts will be in vain. You are not to go to the monasteries or to the Himalayas; you are not to escape from where you are. You have to become awakened where you are.

Worry

Worries are leaks, holes. Worries and anxieties go on dissipating your energy, and overflowing energy is needed to be drunk with the divine.

Drop worrying. There is nothing to worry about; everything is taken care of. Live with that trust. Existence loves you. No harm is going to come to you, no harm can ever come to you, because how can the whole do any harm to its own part? It is impossible. And if sometimes you feel that some harm *is* coming to you, then it must be some misinterpretation on your part; there must be some blessing in disguise.

Worship

'Worship' means wonder, awe, love – not any formal ritual. Going to a temple and worshipping a statue, that is not what is meant by worship. Worship is a new vision, a new insight into reality.

When a child looks at the sun rising, look into his eyes – that is worship. He is so mystified, in such awe. When a child looks at the starry night, look into his eyes, those stars reflected in his eyes – that is worship.

A child knows what worship is. We have forgotten, because we have forgotten the language of wonder. We have become too knowledgeable. When the sun rises, we know what it is. We don't really know, but we have been to school, to college, to university, so we have become knowledgeable. When a flower blooms, we know its name, the species it belongs to and the country it comes from. But all these things are meaningless, irrelevant. We think we know a flower just by giving it a name, but we miss the wonder of it. With the language of wonder, each flower will give a thrill to your heart, each star will give it a new beat and each bird will start singing within you.

Life is so psychedelic, it is full of splendour. To feel the wonder of it, to feel the awe, is worship. And then in some unknown moment you may bow down to existence. You may kneel down on the earth, or you may fall on the sand, in great prayer, in great love, as if the Earth is your mother. And it is. Existence is your mother. And great love will surge up in you. That upsurging love is worship.

Wounds

The mind is a hoarder of bitterness. It collects sounds, hurts, insults. It goes on sulking for years.

Psychologists are very aware of the fact that something said when you were only four years old may have hurt you so much that it is still there like a wound, still oozing pus, years later. You don't allow it to be healed. You go on fingering the wound so you make it hurt again and again. Again and again you create it, never giving it an opportunity to heal by itself. If we look at our mind, it is nothing but wounds. So life becomes a hell; we collect only thorns.

A man may have been loving to you for years, he may have been compassionate, kind and everything, and he says just one thing which hurts you, and years of love and friendship disappear. That one thing becomes more important, weighs more than all that he has done over the years. You forget all his love and his friendship and all his sacrifices for you. You remember that one thing – and you would like to take revenge.

This is the way of the mind. It is a very ugly way. The mind has no grace. Go beyond the mind and you go beyond all bitterness. And the more you surpass the mind, the more your life becomes sweet, as sweet as honey.

Meditation is sweet, the mind is bitter. Move from the mind to meditation. Once you know what meditation is, once you know how you can be without the mind, then you can use the mind and mind cannot use you. That is the moment when the miracle happens, when the rebellion happens, when the fragrance is released.

Wrong

Freedom basically means, intrinsically means, that you are capable of choosing either right or wrong.

And the danger is – and hence the fear – that it is always easier to choose wrong. The wrong is a downhill task and the right is an uphill task. Going uphill is difficult, arduous; and the higher you go, the more arduous it becomes. But going downhill is very easy; you need not do anything, gravity does everything for you. You can just roll like a rock from the top of the hill to the very bottom. But if you want to rise in consciousness, if you want to rise in the world of beauty, truth, bliss, rise to the highest peaks, then that certainly is difficult …

Freedom gives you the opportunity either to fall below the animals or to rise above the angels. Freedom is a ladder: one side of the ladder reaches hell, the other side touches heaven. It is the same ladder; the choice is yours, you choose the direction. You have the freedom to choose.

XYZ

Every art has to reach the point where technology is dropped. Every meditation has to reach the point where methods are dropped. They are good for beginners, for learning the ABCs, but when you have reached the point of XYZ, they are no use.

Silently, you are filled with music. Without moving, you are dancing. Without any thought, any feeling in you, there is just pure grace, gratitude arising out of you, just like fragrance arising out of a lotus flower.

You have to reach this point. Only then have you fulfilled your destiny.

Yes

This simple word contains all the religions of the world. It contains trust, it contains love, it contains surrender. It contains all the prayers that have ever been said, are being said and will ever be said. If you can say 'yes'·with all your heart, you have said all that can be said. To say 'yes' to existence is to be religious, to say 'no' is to be irreligious.

That's my definition of the atheist and the theist. The atheist is not one who denies God and the theist is not one who believes in God – not necessarily so, because we have seen great theists who never believed in God and tremendously enlightened people who never talked about God. But they talked about yes; they had to talk about yes.

God can be dropped as an unnecessary hypothesis, but yes cannot be dropped. Yes is the very spirit of godliness. And yes can exist without God, but God cannot exist without yes. God is only the body, yes is the soul.

There are people who believe in God and yet I will call them atheists, because their belief has no yes behind it. Their belief is bogus, their belief is formal, their belief is given by others, it is borrowed. Their parents, priests and teachers have taught them that God exists; they have made them so afraid that they cannot even question the existence of God. And they have given them promises of great things if they believe in God. There will be great rewards in heaven if you believe and great punishments in hell if you don't believe. Fear and greed have been exploited. The priest has behaved with the congregation almost like the psychologist behaves with the rats upon which he experiments. The rats are controlled by punishment and reward. Reward them, and they start learning the thing for which they are rewarded; punish them, and they start unlearning the thing for which they are punished ...

Theists, atheists, both are victims. The really religious person has nothing to do with the Bible or the Koran or the *Bhagavad Gita*. The really religious person has a deep communion with existence. He can say yes to a rose flower, he can say yes to the stars, he can say yes to people, he can say yes to his own being, to his own desires. He can say yes to whatever life brings him; he is a yea-sayer.

And in this yea-saying is contained the essential prayer.

Yin/Yang

Have you seen the Chinese symbol of yin and yang? Two fish in a circle, one fish in one half-circle, the other fish in the other half-circle; but both fish fitting together, making it a whole. Yin is the feminine; yang is the masculine.

This is applicable to all polarities, positive and negative; they are just like two fish moving in such a way, so closely, that they make a circle.

Then you look at existence with the eyes of a religious person. Then there is no saint, no sinner; they are complementary to each other. They are both needed in some way. And ways can be found so that they can complement each other more lucidly, more gracefully, more beautifully.

Yoga

First, yoga is not a religion, remember that. Yoga is a pure science just like mathematics, physics or chemistry. If Christians discovered the laws of physics, that does not mean that physics is Christian. Physics remains just a science. Yoga is a science too. It is just an accident that Hindus discovered it. It is not Hindu. It is pure science, pure mathematics of the inner being ...

The greatest name as far as the world of yoga is concerned is Patanjali. No one else compares to him. Patanjali was an enlightened person like Buddha, like Krishna, like Christ, like Mahavira, Mohammed, Zarathustra, but he was different from them in one way. Buddha, Krishna, Mahavira, Zarathustra and Mohammed were great founders of religions. They changed the whole pattern of the human mind, but their approach was not scientific.

Patanjali was like an Einstein in the world of Buddhas. He was a phenomenon. He could have easily been a Nobel Prize winner like an Einstein or Bohr or Max Planck, Heisenberg. He had the same attitude, the same rigorous scientific approach. He was not a poet; Krishna was a poet. He was not a moralist; Mahavira was a moralist. He was basically a scientist, thinking in terms of laws. And he formulated the absolute laws of the human being, the ultimate working structure of the human mind and reality.

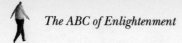

Yoga is concerned with your total being, with your roots. So with Patanjali you will be trying to know the ultimate laws of being: the laws of transformation, the laws of how to die and how to be reborn again, the laws of a new order of being. That is why I call yoga a science.

Zen

Zen is just Zen. There is nothing comparable to it. It is unique – unique in the sense that it is the most ordinary and yet the most extraordinary phenomenon that has ever happened to human consciousness. It is the most ordinary because it does not believe in knowledge, it does not believe in the mind. It is not a philosophy, not a religion either. It is the total acceptance of ordinary existence. It has no interest in any esoteric nonsense, no interest in metaphysics at all. It does not hanker for the other shore; this shore is more than enough. Its acceptance of this shore is so tremendous that through that very acceptance it transforms this shore – and this very shore becomes the other shore.

This very body the Buddha.

This very Earth the lotus paradise.

Zero

Do you know Buddhism disappeared from India in just 500 years? The greatest man in the history of religion, and his religion could not survive for even 500 years. Something was basically wrong in his approach. It was not that he had not realized the truth. He *had* realized the truth, but he was telling people things which he should not have told them. He was telling the truth, but the people were not ready to hear the truth; they wanted a sweet lie. He should have told a sweet lie in such a way that they could swallow the bitter truth with it too. Every truth has to be sugar-coated, otherwise you cannot swallow it.

Buddha said to people, 'When you come to your inner-most point, you will disappear, *anatta* – no self, no being, no soul. You will be just a zero, and the zero will melt into the universal zero.' This is very close to the ultimate truth, but presented in a very crude way. Who wants to become a zero? People want to find eternal bliss. They are tired, miserable, in deep anguish, suffering all kinds of insanity. And they come to the master and the master says, 'The only medicine is that you become a zero' – in other words, the disease can be cured only if the patient is killed. Translated exactly, that is what it means. Well, naturally the disease will disappear when the patient is killed, but you had come to be cured, not to be killed. No wonder the religion disappeared within five centuries. People did not find it tasteful, alluring or attractive. It was naked and true, but who wants naked truth?

I have to talk about bliss, about benediction, about thousands of lotuses blossoming in you. If thousands of lotuses bloom inside you, thousands of suns rise, then you will think that it is worth it to find one hour in 24 to just sit silently.

But the truth is, no lotuses, no suns – just pure nothing-ness.

That's what Gautama Buddha was telling people.

But anything that has been said or can be said is just an indication, a finger pointing. Look at what the finger is pointing at – the unknowable, the mysterious – and move …

Zorba the Buddha

The past has created a split in mankind; there is a constant civil war in every human being. If you do not feel at ease, the reason is not personal. The disease is social.

The strategy that has been used is to divide you into two enemy camps: the Zorba the Greek and Gautama the Buddha, the materialist and the spiritualist.

You are not divided in reality. In reality you are a harmonious whole. But you are conditioned to think that you are not one whole and that if you want to be a spiritual being, you have to fight your body, you have to conquer, defeat, destroy, torture it in every possible way.

I would like you to be Zorba *and* Gautama, simultaneously. Less than that won't do. Zorba represents the Earth with all its flowers and greenery and mountains and rivers and oceans. Buddha represents the sky with all its stars and clouds and rainbows.

The sky without the Earth will be empty. The sky cannot laugh without the Earth. The Earth without the sky will be dead. Put them both together and a dance comes into existence. The Earth and the sky dance together, and there is laughter, there is joy, there is celebration.

INDEX